MiG Alley to Mu Ghia Pass

MiG Alley to Mu Ghia Pass

Memoirs of a Korean War Ace

by CECIL G. FOSTER

with DAVID K. VAUGHAN

FOREWORD BY DOLPH OVERTON

McFarland & Company, Inc., Publishers
Jefferson, North Carolina, and London

Library of Congress Cataloguing-in-Publication Data

Foster, Cecil G., 1925–
    MiG alley to Mu Ghia pass : memoirs of a Korean war ace / by
Cecil G. Foster with David K. Vaughan ; foreword by Dolph Overton.
        p.   cm.
    Includes index.
    ISBN 0-7864-0995-9 (softcover : 60# alkaline paper) ∞
    1. Foster, Cecil G., 1925– 2. Fighter pilots—United States—
Biography.   3. United States. Air Force—Biography.   I. Vaughan,
David Kirk.   II. Title.
UG626.2.F67 A3   2001
951.904'2—dc21   2001031263
[B]

British Library cataloguing data are available

Manufactured in the United States of America

McFarland & Company, Inc., Publishers
    Box 611, Jefferson, North Carolina 28640
      www.mcfarlandpub.com

Table of Contents

Foreword

Dolph Overton,
16th Fighter Interceptor Squadron,
51st Fighter Interceptor Wing

Dolphin ("Dolph") Overton was an ace in the 16th Fighter Squadron. He had the amazing record of shooting down five MiGs in the final four days of his tour of duty in Korea. Dolph Overton shot down his fourth and fifth MiGs during the same days Cecil Foster shot down his eighth and ninth. He eventually returned to his southern roots in North Carolina.

A FTER FLYING A TOUR in F-84s with the 49th Fighter Bomber Group at K-2 (Taegu), where I was operations officer of the 8th Squadron, I was allowed to fly a tour in F-86s. I reported to the 16th Squadron of the 51st Fighter Group in September, 1952. Cecil was already an old-timer in the squadron at that point. He had been there two months! He had shown his prowess and had four MiGs to his credit. He was made flight commander when still a first lieutenant (which was unusual), and very soon he was promoted to captain. Not long after that I too was made a flight commander. At this point I got to know Cecil much better. As two of the 16th's four flight commanders, we spent a lot of time together and became close friends. Cecil got his fifth MiG on November 22nd to become an ace. I was still hunting.

Cecil, although from Michigan, did not talk much faster than I, and could have passed for a southerner. He was physically fit, solid, tough, and seemed to have ice water in his veins. He was serious most of the time, had natural leadership qualities, and held the respect of everyone. He was protective of the members of his flight and spent an unusual amount of time coaching them and others like me, who had no claims of victories over the MiGs.

He was one of the most decent people I ever met. He never used a cuss word, did not drink or spend time at the club, but always had time for his flight personnel. He was not, perhaps, the model of the "hot rock" pilot depicted in the movies, but he was very effective in combat when the chips were down.

There were periods when there was no air activity by the MiGs. Later, after the war, we analyzed the cycles of activity and inactivity. Weather was a factor, as was the rotation of Russian squadrons to the Korean front. Also, there was the in-commission rate, which was a measure of how many planes were mechanically ready to fly. Sometimes the MiGs just did not leave China. You cannot shoot a plane down if it does not fly when you are flying or does not fly into your combat zone. During those inactive times some pilots ventured across the Yalu River into China hoping to engage in enemy activity. Cecil never crossed the Yalu illegally.

Eisenhower was inaugurated as president on January 23, 1953. For several days before that date and during the following week, the MiGs, after a long period of low activity, made a daily show of force. After that long dry spell of enemy inactivity, our flights were ready and well rehearsed. I got my fifth and Cecil got his eighth and ninth. We flew our last missions, finished our tours, checked out of the squadron, and headed home together.

We stopped in Tokyo where we were debriefed. While processing out and before heading back to the States, we got haircuts. I had the barber shave off my "good luck" mustache. We were in a crowded downtown Tokyo barber shop and Cecil had asked me not to leave without him. I finished first and was standing by the door. Cecil soon was finished, stood up, looked directly at me and said, "Where is that Overton? He promised not to leave without me." My appearance without my old "Stalin" type of mustache was so completely different that he did not know me. We eventually made it back to the States.

We did not see each other again for forty-five years. When we did meet, I recognized him immediately. He had changed very little. He was still the same quiet, unassuming, great guy I had known in that other world, in another era. Both our eyes were watery as we gave each other an embrace that spoke for our hearts. Though there had been a lot of water under the bridge, the memories of the experiences we shared had hardly faded.

Preface

David K. Vaughan

CECIL FOSTER JOINED the Army Air Force in 1943 as a private and retired in 1975 as a lieutenant colonel. During the 32 years that he was associated with the Air Force, he was a celestial navigator, radar-navigator-bombardier, pilot, intercept director, and squadron commander. He flew jet aircraft in Alaska, Korea, North Africa, Europe, Vietnam, and across the breadth of the United States. Success did not come easily to Cecil. Raised in the north-central section of Michigan, he early suffered the loss of his mother and the disintegration of his nuclear family. Surviving economic and emotional hardships in his youth, he entered the service at the height of the American World War II buildup. Believing that the navigator's task was more challenging, because a higher test score was required to become a navigator, he initially trained as a navigator. Later he earned his radar-navigator-bombardier rating and was serving as a radar-navigator instructor as the war ended.

Serving as navigator taught him that although navigators might be smarter than pilots (according to the standardized test scores, anyway), it was the pilot who flew the airplane. Cecil applied for pilot training and was accepted. He survived pilot training at a time when the military services were undergoing a severe reduction in force after the war. But he persevered and was rewarded by graduating as a member of the first pilot training class to be commissioned as Air Force, not Army, officers. He was fortunate also in that he received a few hours of jet time in the then-new P-80 aircraft (forerunner of the F-80 and later, the T-33). But his luck seemed to run out when, after being assigned to a squadron in Alaska, and

1

paying out of his own pocket to bring his wife and family to Alaska to join him, he was notified that he had been selected for release from the service.

Cecil struggled valiantly to survive as a civilian, first in Michigan and then in Texas. When the Korean War began, Cecil saw an opportunity to do the one job he had learned to love—fly airplanes for the Air Force. But the Air Force had apparently lost Cecil's personnel and flying records, which repeatedly frustrated his attempts to rejoin. Finally he was brought back into the Air Force in August 1951, but as a navigator, not a pilot. This minor problem did not deter Cecil, however, and he was eventually able to convince the Air Force to reinstate his status as a pilot.

He was sent to Nellis Air Force Base to train in the F-86, and promptly transferred to Korea, where he joined the 16th Fighter Squadron in the 51st Fighter Interceptor Wing. The 51st had just been installed to assist the 4th FIW, which had been flying F-86s against MiG-15s for over a year. Cecil arrived in the 16th in late May of 1952. By November he was an ace, the 23rd American ace of the war. Cecil's accounts of how he repeatedly engaged with the enemy when the opportunity presented itself provide lessons in the characteristics of a good fighter pilot. As his story shows, it's not daring or foolhardiness that count, but nerve, determination, and skill. When he left Korea in January 1953, he was credited with nine MiG kills. He returned to a hero's welcome in San Antonio, and to his wife Margaret and their four boys.

He next flew F-86Ds for Air Defense Command, first at Perrin AFB Texas, and then at Westover AFB, Massachusetts. In 1958, the entire unit was transferred to Sidi Slimaine, Morocco. In 1960 he was transferred to Great Falls, Montana, this time as a weapons director in the SAGE radar control system. Once again, however, Cecil was able to return to the cockpit—this time in an F-101. Then, after a pleasant interlude at Ramstein, Germany, where he was Chief of Fighter Operations and then Commandant of the Air-Ground Operations School, he was sent to Da Nang, South Vietnam, flying the F-4D in air-to-ground attack missions. As squadron commander of the 390th Tactical Fighter Squadron, from 1968 to 1969, he flew nearly 170 combat missions. On two of those missions, his aircraft was severely damaged. In one instance he was able to return and land safely, but the second time, he and his back-seater had to bail out of their aircraft. Fortunately, both were safely recovered.

Cecil served for seven more years after returning from Vietnam. He flew F-101s once again, and then after that unit was phased out, he transferred to McChord AFB for the final assignment of his Air Force career. When he retired, on 1 July 1975, he had accumulated over 5000 hours of flying time and had earned twenty-five medals and decorations, including two Silver Stars, three Distinguished Flying Crosses, the Bronze Star, the Purple Heart, two Meritorious Service Medals, thirteen Air Medals, the Air Force Commendation Medal, Chungmoo Medal for Military Merit with Silver Star from the South Korean president and the Republic of Vietnam Gold Cross for Gallantry with Gold Star.

In reviewing Cecil's career, two aspects stand out clearly: the first and most obvious is that he had to make many of his own breaks. In primary training, he practically taught himself to fly. He processed his paperwork himself when he was forced to leave the Air Force after World War II, and it was through sheer determination that he was able to re-enter active service during the Korean War and change his assignment from navigator-bombardier to pilot. In spite of the occasional inertia of the Air Force personnel management system, he made a successful career for himself.

The other aspect that stands out clearly is his belief in thoroughly training his wingmen. Whether as a flight commander in Korea or a squadron commander in Vietnam, he taught those with whom he worked most closely how to be leaders themselves. In times and environments when leadership was often discussed more than it was practiced, he established training programs designed to give those with whom he flew and worked the opportunity to recognize the important tasks that needed to be done and the skills with which to accomplish those tasks. His success in showing others how to succeed is demonstrated by the number of officers who worked for him who later achieved general officer rank.

A modest man, especially for a fighter pilot, Cecil never let his ego interfere with his common sense and his concern for the physical and professional well-being of all men in his unit. His story is as instructive as it is exciting, and I am proud to have played a part in bringing it to fruition.

CHAPTER 1

My Early Days
in Michigan

I CONSIDER MYSELF LUCKY to have survived my early childhood. Maybe the stamina and endurance I displayed helped me to become a successful fighter pilot later in life. At the time, of course, I thought my life was like everyone else's. I was born the 30th day of August, 1925, in a farmhouse in Midland County, Michigan. My mother, Alma Cecile Tippin, and my father, Christian Everett Foster, always known by the name of Everett, lived on a ten-acre farm where they farmed and produced enough food, at least for a few years, to take care of our needs. There were three older sisters, Esther, Beulah (who preferred the nickname of Niki), and Frances, and two younger brothers, Arthur and Robert. When I was quite young a tri-motor airplane, possibly one of the early Ford Motor Company trimotor aircraft, landed near our farm, and my father took me over to look at it. The pilot was giving rides for a fee like the early barnstormers used to do. But we couldn't afford to pay for rides and I had to be content with looking.

I don't recall many of the events of those early years. Once, when we didn't have enough food to eat, my mother went to our next door neighbor's farmhouse and volunteered to help them shell corn using a corn-shelling machine. This hand-cranked machine stripped the hardened kernels of corn off the cob and dumped them into a large wooden box. There would always be a few kernels of corn remaining at the small end of the corncob. My mother volunteered to do this work for my neighbor for the opportunity to take the stripped corncobs home and shell off the remaining kernels of corn to feed us. My mother died before I turned six. She had attended a religious revival meeting in the neighboring town of Breckenridge. The meeting was held under a large tent with long wooden benches and wood chips covering the ground; people sat down on those benches a good part of the day listening to the religious messages given by the evangelists. My mother apparently was exposed to the germ of poliomyelitis, also known as infantile paralysis. After we returned home she was struck with polio and wasn't able to breathe. The local doctor said there was nothing he could do; he called Saginaw General Hospital and an ambulance was sent out—but it looked more like a hearse to me. I can vividly recall somebody lifting me up so I could see my mother lying down in the back of this vehicle. They told me that might be the last time I would ever see her. I didn't realize how sick she was. She died soon after. A series of housekeepers came in to take care of us kids for a while.

Once in a while my father could get work in the oil fields that had been drilled in the area, working for fifty cents an hour, which was pretty good money in those days. But the work was occasional and did not provide enough money for us to live on. I started attending school in a one-room schoolhouse, located about three-quarters of a mile from our house. During that first winter I walked to and from school along a road with a deep ditch running alongside, probably eight or nine feet deep, used for drainage; I was afraid I might lose my footing and fall in. Eventually my father couldn't find work in the oil fields and had no money to pay for housekeepers. One housekeeper used her own money to buy food for us, but finally she told my father that she just couldn't help us out any longer—she needed the money for herself.

My father was forced to rely on other family members for assistance. He placed the three older sisters and me with my maternal grandparents, Grandpa and Grandma Crabb. My next younger brother, Arthur, was placed with a family that owned a large farm. My youngest brother, Robert, was taken in by my father's sister, Jenny. While I lived at Grandpa Crabb's farm I once again attended a one-room school house located about a mile and a half distant, walking to school past the Dow Chemical Company's brine wells which pumped underground salt water up to the surface.

One of our neighboring families was named Eastman. One day there was a horrible fire, and Grandpa Crabb went over to help save the animals stabled in the barn. The barn was burning on both ends, but the fire hadn't spread to the middle section. I watched my grandpa leading the horses out of the barn; the horses were so scared they were rearing up and whinnying, and he put a coat over their eyes so they couldn't see the flames. While the men were busy in the barn, someone called out that the house was on fire. One of the Eastman children had set fires at both ends of the barn, and while the family was putting the fire out in the barn and getting the animals out, he lit two more fires on the far side of the house. They put out the fires near the house before it was engulfed in flames, but the barn burned to the ground.

I became ill with scarlet fever; I was so ill that my grandparents thought I might die, and they contacted my father. My father came by to see me in the room where I was kept isolated from the rest of the family and handed me three oranges he had brought with him. Eventually I recovered, but it was a slow process; when I first tried to sit up in bed I became so dizzy I had to lie down again. After a while, I regained my strength and was able to return to school. I lived with my maternal grandparents for about two years until my grandmother became too ill to take care of us. Once again we were split up; one sister lived with an aunt, another worked as a maid; my eldest sister decided to marry.

My father took me to his parents' farm, about seven miles southeast of Mt. Pleasant. The farm was a reasonably prosperous farm. Grandfather Foster had horses, cows, hogs, chickens, and ducks, and I learned to gather eggs, feed the chickens, clean the stalls for the cattle, and do all the chores that have to be done on a farm. It wasn't an easy life. I spent my time working or studying, and there were no other children around to play with. I learned to raise all sorts of good farm products for eating, like corn and beans and lettuce, and I learned how to take care of the apple trees and pear trees. I helped my grandmother can peas and beans. I milked the cows, and after we separated the cream from the milk, I churned the cream by hand to make butter. There were many tasks around the farm that I learned to do, and I became quite self-reliant. These experiences helped me later in life; I learned early not to depend on anyone else. If something needed to be done, I'd do it myself. I rarely saw any of my siblings. Rarely did we all get together. It was a lonely time; I never had the opportunity to really get to know my brothers and sisters very well because I was raised in isolation.

When I lived with my paternal grandparents, the schoolhouse I attended was a mile and three-quarters away if I walked by the shortest route. If I went to school the long way, it was two and a quarter miles distant. I walked or ran to school to improve my breathing capacity. Some other physical problems occurred while I lived with my paternal grandparents. As a result of one illness I experienced one summer, I couldn't take a deep breath because it hurt to do so. My weakened condition never seemed to improve, and I finally decided that I was just going to have to work through it, which I did. Eventually I started running from the farm to the school to build up my lungs. I believe it was a successful therapeutic effort on my part, and I did it without anybody telling me what to do. I've never had a problem since. Later the doctors told me that I might have had rheumatic fever, for something gave me a first degree heart block, which was discovered in 1957, when I was examined for my Regular Air Force commission physical.

When I was living with Grandpa and Grandma Foster, we had some of the most severe winters imaginable. The snow was unusually deep and the drifts on the road were higher than my head. It was so cold we could walk on top of the snow. The snow-covered surface gave a roller coaster effect; we could walk up one side and slide down the other on the roads to school. No snow plows came to clear our roads, and my uncle, who drove to work with his old automobile, was able to drive on top of these waves of snow and go back and forth to work. I've never seen anything like it since.

After I had been living with my paternal grandparents for about two years, my grandfather had a stroke; he was paralyzed on one side and couldn't walk or do any of the work that had to be done around the farm. I did as many of the farm chores as I could, but because I was only eleven years old I just wasn't able to do the larger tasks. I helped to take care of my grandfather; I shaved him, washed him, and helped him dress and move about in a wheel chair. Some nights he would go into a critical condition and start chewing on his tongue and experience other control problems. My grandmother would wake me up and I would run down to my Uncle Marion Foster's house, a little over a half mile away, in the black of night. I was scared to death, running down this road, because the trees and bushes along the road all seemed to be alive. When I arrived at his house I had to be especially careful, because he owned some really mean dogs. I would climb the fence, run across the yard, rap on the window, and get back out to the fence before the dogs knew I was there. Eventually, between my rapping on the window and the dogs' barking, Uncle Marion would get up and come out to the farm to help my grandmother take care of my grandfather.

While I lived with my grandparents I went to a one-room school from the fourth through the eighth grade. There were thirty to thirty-five students in all eight grades; there were five in my class. After I graduated from the eighth grade I attended high school in the town of Shepherd, which was six or seven miles from our house. I rode the bus to school in my freshman year. My grandmother gradually sold everything to provide money for eating and living expenses. She sold the car, the horses, the cows, and the farm machinery. We ate the chickens. Life became difficult for us. In about five years' time we lost the farm because we couldn't pay the taxes, and we had to move out. At the end of my freshman year my grandparents had to move to Shepherd; both had no income except a small old age pension. But they couldn't pay the house rent, so we had to move again. This time we moved to Mt. Pleasant, and I was able to find a ride to Shepherd to finish the last six weeks of the first semester of my sophomore year.

I started school in Mt. Pleasant the second semester of my sophomore year. About two months later, my grandmother got up one morning, apparently became dizzy, fell, struck her head on a bedpost, went into a coma, and never recovered. She died soon after. I finished the rest of that semester in a travel trailer that my father placed in the Mt. Pleasant city park. At the end of my sophomore year my father and I moved to Midland. Later my father remarried Esther Syckle, a woman from the Midland area, and I was able to have a room in their garage. My brother Arthur joined me and the two of us shared this room in the garage through my last two years in high school. I attended three different high schools: Shepherd, Mt. Pleasant, and Midland. I finished the eleventh and twelfth grades and graduated from Midland High School in June of 1943.

While I was in the ninth grade at Shepherd, I played intramural football. I wanted to play sports all my life, but most of the time I had to work and I was unable to participate in sports activities. When I attended Midland High School, I had the opportunity to go out for the track team, and I lettered in track in my senior year. I also was injured playing a game similar to football and ripped all the ligaments in my right foot. I was on crutches for about seven weeks. If I put my ankle on an angle, for instance, to walk on the side of a hill, that foot hurt badly. This injury bothered me for some time. However, when I took my physical to enter the Army Air Corps, this problem was not detected.

I was in my stepmother's home when we learned of the Japanese attack at Pearl Harbor. About five o'clock in the afternoon, a newsboy ran down our street yelling, "Extra, Extra, Japanese attack Hawaii." This attack was a shock to everyone in the community. I hadn't been following world news, but I knew that Hitler was taking over most of Europe. America was neutral, and had no intention of becoming involved, at least that was what the papers said, but when the Japanese attack came, attitudes soon changed. I was still in school, two years away from graduation, and we had some hard days from then on, because all items were rationed. We bought everything with ration stamps, from gasoline to shoes to clothes to food. We had to have stamps to buy an item, and if we didn't have stamps, we didn't buy it.

I worked as a gas station attendant to earn money, and I learned many things about vehicles I hadn't known before. I also worked in a bowling alley as a pin boy. I learned how to set pins in two alleys at the same time and was able to double my pay, which still was low. I earned four cents a line to set pins, so I could make 50 or 75 cents in an evening. I worked as a gardener around town for the families that were a little more well-to-do. My farm background enabled me to tend to their flowers with some success; I cut grass and trimmed shrubs. I didn't have time for athletics.

In general, I earned good grades throughout high school. I think my average was about a B or B+, and I filled the necessary requirements for the college preparatory sequence. However, that plan never worked out, because I knew that as soon as I graduated, I would be drafted. I didn't attend many high school class functions, because during that time there wasn't much to do. Everything was rationed during the war, and most of the usual school functions were canceled. I did learn to drive an automobile. There wasn't much to it in those days. I just climbed into the family car and drove it. I don't remember when I received my license. Between my junior and senior year, a friend and I drove up to Traverse City where we spent two weeks picking cherries. That was one of the few times I ever left the Midland area.

When the war started for America, my father told me he didn't want me to be a foot soldier; he said that was not the way to go to war, and said I should join the Army Air Force. He drove with me to Battle Creek to enlist me in the Army Air Corps aviation cadet program. I passed the written and physical examinations, and on 12 August 1943 I was sworn in as a private in the enlisted reserve corps, committed, as the phrase on my papers said, to serve "for the duration plus six months." I was told to go home and wait for orders placing me on active duty. The officials in Battle Creek told me I should report to the draft board on my birthday, as I was supposed to do, but I should show them a little card that indicated that I was a private in the enlisted reserve corps. Then the local draft board wouldn't be able to draft me. When my birthday came around, I did as they said and I'll tell you I've never seen so many mad people in my life, because Midland was having a terrible time meeting the draft quota. When I walked in and showed my card, the man behind the counter said, "That card doesn't make any difference. You're going to go to Detroit tomorrow to be drafted," and I said, "No, this man in Battle Creek said you can't do that." For about 45 minutes they went through all the books they could find, and they found out that yes, this lieutenant who enlisted me was right. They were really upset because they could not draft me. And now I was an aviation cadet in the Army.

CHAPTER 2

World War II Training

I SUPPOSE MY WORLD War II training experiences were no different than those of thousands of other men at the time, but if theirs were the same as mine, then our training experiences should have taught us all to prepare for the unexpected and to expect a hard road to combat. In October of 1943 I was ordered to report to Rockford, Illinois. To reach Rockford I had to take a train through Chicago, and I'd never been to Chicago. What a city! It was huge, bigger than anything I'd ever seen before. I received help finding the train to Rockford from people in the Chicago train terminal. I stood right by it until we were allowed to board. When we arrived in Rockford, a few men in uniform accompanied us to the camp, where they showed us how to make a military bed and how to scrub and clean everything from the day room to the sleeping quarters, which were big, open-bay areas, to the latrine, to the orderly room—anything to keep us busy for three days.

A sergeant directed us to put our clothes in a box for shipment home. I was paid for my travel expenses from Midland to Rockford, and given a uniform which didn't fit very well. But it was something to wear. In the middle of the night we were ordered to get up, get dressed, and then marched in a loose formation down to the train station, where we boarded a train again. After sitting there for hours, we moved out of the station. Three days later we arrived at Jefferson Barracks, Missouri, to begin our basic training. We lived in huts with wooden floors and wooden walls; there were cracks in the walls, between half and three quarters of an inch wide, and the tops were canvas. In the middle of the room was a pot-bellied stove. There were double bunks along the sides and the ends to accommodate the maximum number of people. Winter was approaching, and spinal meningitis struck a number of men in the area where I was bivouacked;

11

the medics hauled us out in ambulances. One night the ambulances carried nineteen people away. I never heard what happened to them. I was one of the fortunate few who didn't get the disease. But I developed an ear infection which bothered me for several weeks.

Before we graduated from the basic training area we were given some special examinations, called psychomotor exams, for the aviation cadet program. If we couldn't pass these, we were eliminated from the cadet program; this was the first of the "washout" opportunities that occurred while we were in basic training. Psychomotor tests involved hand-eye adeptness and coordination, hearing, and reaction capabilities. In one of these tests, we had to hold an electrode over a dot that appeared on a circular, spinning plate. The plate was set off center, so that it would appear to wobble as the plates spun around, and we had to keep holding it on the dot. The instructors measured the length of time we were able to keep the electrode over this small dot. If we didn't have the ability to hold it in place, we were removed from the program. There were other similar types of exams.

Those of us who passed these tests were issued new cadet uniforms and ordered to report to our next station, which was the College Training Detachment, or CTD. I was sent to Knox College, in Galesburg, Illinois. After I arrived in Galesburg, my ear began to ache again. When I went on sick call the doctor looked at my ear, grabbed an instrument, reached inside my ear, and pulled out a green wad of cotton. He said, "How long has this been in your ear?" I said, "I don't know. I went on sick call in Jefferson Barracks about six weeks ago or maybe longer." When I had gone on sick call at Jefferson Barracks, apparently the doctor had inserted some medicine on a wad of cotton and never told me to go back to have it taken out. The doctor laughed to think I had been carrying a wad of cotton in my ear for two months.

While I was stationed in Galesburg I flew for the first time in the flight indoctrination program. For a three-week period, from the middle of April through the first week of May 1944, I accumulated ten hours of flying time in an Aeronca Champ, a small two-place aircraft, in which I received instruction from a civilian instructor pilot. This was a pleasant change of pace from the monotonous routine of drill and academics. It was my first time in an airplane and although I was understandably nervous, I enjoyed the experience tremendously. But just as I was beginning to feel like I could handle the aircraft myself, the flight instruction period ended.

While we were in CTD there was an emergency in Europe. An order came directing anyone who had received basic training in any of the branches of the Army besides the aviation cadet training to be immediately removed from the aviation cadet program and to report for immediate shipment to Europe. This may have been due to the buildup of men required for the invasion of Europe, which took place on June 6th, 1944, or possibly for the heavy action which was taking place in Italy. Many of the cadets were gone within twelve hours. It was a traumatic experience. One of my best friends in the training program, who had been a corporal in the army, was told that he had to leave the program and go to Europe. Before he left, he and I went into a bar about a block and a half from where we were living to have a farewell party. It was the first and only time I ever got completely, disgustingly drunk. We didn't do anything wrong, just got drunk, so drunk I couldn't even stand up straight. I never did that again. I never did find out what happened to my friend after he left for Europe.

In the cadet program we received "gigs," or demerits, for dust in our rooms or for not having a haircut or when our shoes weren't shined or when we didn't stand up straight during inspection. When we received a specified number of "gigs" we walked a tour, an hour of marching back and forth with a rifle on our shoulders. Nobody wanted to march a tour, so we worked hard to keep up our appearances and the appearances of our rooms. It was a tough way to learn discipline, but it worked. While we were in CTD we had to stand guard duty. We seldom were allowed to leave the post and had little time to socialize. My father and his brother Ommer visited me once, and my sister Nikki also came to visit while I was at Galesburg.

Once we completed CTD, we hoped to go directly into training, but we were told there were no openings in the cadet program, and as a result we were sent to what was called "on-the-line training" at Aloe Army Air Field, near Victoria, Texas. There we were given little make-work details until the next available aviation cadet training class began. While we were there, we watched the cadets in flight training. The cadets who graduated and were commissioned went into advanced training in P-40s. We used to watch them on their graduation day exercise to see how many people had accidents. Once two planes ran into one another overhead, inside the field boundaries, and we watched the parachutes open when the student pilots bailed out. We didn't have trouble keeping busy. We learned how to refuel the aircraft, clean the windscreens, and polish the propellers. We'd pick up papers around the base and do other things. If there was nothing else to do, they gave us a cloth and told us to clean the airplanes. Eventually they found room for us in the aviation cadet program in the summer of 1944.

We went to the San Antonio Aviation Cadet Center, the SAACC, for additional examinations and preflight training. There we were administered the Stanine tests. Stanine tests evaluated abilities in three categories—

pilot, navigator, and bombardier. The highest score you could get in any one category was a nine, and if you wanted to be a navigator, you had to score a nine; you had to be at the very top if you were going to get into navigation school. If you wanted to be a bombardier you had to score at least a seven. If you wanted to be a pilot, you had to score a level of five. The toughest one to get into was navigation school. Because I didn't know any better, and because I scored nines on all of the tests, I chose navigation school. I thought I was making a smart decision.

I was sent to celestial navigation training at San Marcos, Texas. But before I left San Antonio, I went into town for some off-post relaxation and in the course of visiting there I met a young lady named Margaret Frazar. I visited her often, either at her place or at some location in town. We went to the zoo and attended other civic functions, and she'd come out to the cadet center on weekends now and then. It wasn't long before I realized I had fallen in love with Margaret. When we obtained passes to leave the base at San Marcos on weekends, a bunch of us would go into town and rent a car, drive into San Antonio, and I'd visit Margaret and her friends. On the 13th of January, 1945, Margaret and I were married. I graduated from Aviation Cadets navigator training on the 10th of February and was commissioned a second lieutenant.

After graduating from navigator training, I took Margaret to Michigan to meet my family. We traveled to and from Michigan by bus. Traveling all that distance by bus takes a long time. We didn't stop for hotels, we just got on the bus and rode and dozed or talked. We traveled day and night. It took approximately three days to travel one way. The busses stopped at every major city and we'd have to change busses. But even so, it was a pleasant trip. One day, my dad took us ice fishing. My wife had never been ice fishing in her life. After we dressed her up in layers of winter clothing, you could hardly tell she was human. After my 15-day leave was over, we went back to San Marcos. Soon new orders arrived, assigning me to radar observer bombardier training, "ROB school," at Victorville, California. Margaret and I lived in San Bernardino, and every morning I'd get up and get out on the road about a quarter to five, hitchhiking my way up Cajon Pass along a two-lane road, through the hills. There was always a fog on this road, a big winding road—not at all like it is today. I reached Victorville by six o'clock in the morning, where I reported in to fly or attend ground school. At the end of the day I hitchhiked back to San Bernardino. I did this for three and a half months.

I graduated from ROB school in June; my orders sent me back to Texas, to Pyote Army Air Field. We took a train to San Antonio and then a bus to Pyote. There I was assigned as a flight instructor for crews preparing to go to the Pacific Theater, but I really was not qualified to be a flight instructor, because I'd just graduated from the program. Most of the students who came through the program were as knowledgeable as I was. Later, after about a month, there was an opening for a ground school instructor. I took that position, and I really learned more there than I did in school about the equipment and the procedures of the radar navigator bombardier position. That job gave me an opportunity to teach the radar equipment. I had to really learn it to teach it and that's how I became highly qualified in my job.

Margaret Frazar and Cecil Foster, wedding picture, January 1945.

But then the war in Europe ended, and the field was designated to be closed. As the last officer assigned to the ground school, I was assigned the responsibility for turning in all equipment to the supply section. After the school closed, I was transferred in January 1946 to Grand Island Army Air Field, in Grand Island, Nebraska. My first son—Cecil, Junior—had been born on 27 November 1945. My wife and I and my newborn son, who was only a month old, rode to Grand Island on a train. We had no passenger amenities whatsoever; it was just an open train. What was worse, there was absolutely no heat in it. We traveled during a really cold period in early January. The baby had to have a warm bottle, and we had no way to heat it. As an officer, I could walk to the troop train section, where there was warm water in the rest rooms. I carried the baby bottle up to one of the rest rooms and ran warm water over it until it was somewhat warm. This trip was hazardous for us, because when we arrived in Grand Island, within days my son was in the hospital with pneumonia. We almost lost him. Fortunately, he did recover, but it was a scary time for us.

At Grand Island I was assigned to a B-24 unit that was scheduled to deploy to Alaska. I didn't have any desire to go to Alaska. And by this time

I'd found out about flying airplanes—it didn't make any difference what the Stanine score was, the guy that flew that airplane, the pilot, he was in charge. When I finally learned this profound truth, I said, "Hey, I want to be a pilot." I applied for pilot training and was very happy when I learned I had been accepted.

CHAPTER 3

In the Post-War Air Force

WHILE I WAS AT GRAND ISLAND, I completed 18 months in grade as a second lieutenant, so I recommended myself for promotion to first lieutenant. I did it myself because I was the squadron adjutant and the commander left all administrative actions to me. My promotion was approved before I left for pilot training. My second son, Bryan, was born 10 November 1946, just before I entered primary pilot training. I reported to Randolph Field in January 1947. I purchased a small, 30-foot travel trailer from my father, which we pulled to San Antonio and parked in a trailer court. Several other trainees had the same idea. We lived on the Austin highway, and I drove from there to Randolph Field every day.

I was in primary from March through June of 1947. In primary training I flew the Stearman PT-13D, a sturdy old biplane that was practically indestructible. Soon after I arrived, my instructor became ill, was put in the hospital, and eventually was transferred out. But I was still scheduled to fly. Fortunately, I had flown with him long enough to be cleared to fly solo. I flew my remaining solo missions with a book on my knee. I would fly along, reading the instructions in the book which told me how to do various aerobatic maneuvers—the lazy eight, the chandelle, and turns along a fence line, when I had to correct for the effects of the wind. I read it all out of the book, and then after I'd read it, I'd close the book, put it under my leg, and practice. I essentially taught myself. After we flew a specified number of missions, we were scheduled for our preliminary check rides. When I flew my check ride, I passed all my tests.

I was approaching the time to graduate from primary, but I was short of the required hours of dual flying time, and I flew with any instructor who was available. I maintain that no one helped me learn how to fly; I

17

did that myself. In primary training, the Air Force "washed out" two out of every three trainees. While that was a high rate of failure, the instructors assured us that the one pilot out of three who remained should make it through the next stage of pilot training without difficulty. We felt good when we heard that. Little did we know that that wasn't true.

When we finished primary, we went into basic, where we flew AT-6s. The AT-6, or T-6 as we called it, had previously been used in advanced training and was now used in basic training. In the T-6 program, we had more qualified instructors—people who had come back from the war with a lot of experience. I and two other officers—one was a naval academy graduate and the other was a graduate of West Point—reported to this captain, who told us on the first day that in two weeks only one of the three of us would be left. He said it was too difficult to teach more than one student, and that was all he was going to keep—he was going to "wash out" the other two.

This instructor was a "knee-banger"—if he didn't like how you were flying, or if you didn't do exactly what he told you to do, when he wanted you to do it, he would rap your knees sharply with the control stick. He wasn't the only one to use this technique—other instructors did, too, and we would come back from flying with big purple welts on the insides of our knees. I don't remember getting banged very much, so I guess I must have flown the aircraft pretty well. But sure enough, after two weeks, our class size was reduced until only one out of three was left. Surprisingly, I was still there. But word of the severe attrition reached higher levels.

There was a lieutenant colonel, a navigator, in our group of pilot training students. He had flown in World War II and had previously been assigned to Army Air Force Headquarters in the Pentagon. He called some of his friends at the Pentagon and told them what was going on, that the instructors were wasting government money by washing out students. Two weeks later a headquarters investigation team showed up, and they soon reinstated almost every one who had been eliminated during the basic training phase. These people represented the cream of the crop of applicants, people who had survived elimination in CTD and psychomotor tests, and the other tests. There really weren't very many people left from the original number left to proceed through training.

After the students had been reinstated, the training program continued. I was in basic pilot training from July until the first part of October. During the remainder of my time in pilot training, the only washouts that I knew of were a few of those who had been eliminated earlier and reinstated. We were the second pilot training class to start after the war ended, and we were the first class to graduate as part of the United States Air

Force. Our class consisted of both officers and aviation cadets. The previous class had been part of the United States Army Air Force, but we were the first to graduate as Air Force pilots. We also were the first class in which some students trained in Advanced Pilot Training as jet pilots flying P-80 aircraft. Some of us were trained as reciprocating engine pilots; we flew P-51s. Some of us who started in P-51s were selected for the last month to receive ten hours of jet training. So there were three different categories of pilots in our class.

I was especially fortunate in that I was selected to attend advanced fighter school at Williams Air Force Base, near Phoenix, Arizona, while others were sent to fly B-25s and B-17s. At Williams I flew the P-51 and T-6, and in my last month there, in February of 1948, I flew the P-80, as it was known then. The model we flew did not have drop tanks on the wings, and the airplane was light enough that we had no difficulty landing or taking off from the 5000-foot runway at "Willy Field."

Although we were officers, it didn't make any difference while we were in training. We were still treated as cadets. The nights at Willy Field were cold. We marched down to the flight line in the morning wearing heavy winter clothing as the sun came up, and the water along the sides of the road was frozen. At noon when we were through flying for the day, we would march back from the flight line to ground school, our coats hanging over our shoulders, because it was so warm. While we were at Williams Field, my second son, Bryan, who was one year old, was struck with asthma. When we went to the hospital on the field, the doctors said he had "dust pneumonia." From that time on, he has suffered from asthma. He never was able to outgrow it.

Upon graduation from pilot school, the top people in the class—we were scored in both flying and academic abilities—were able to choose their assignments. Our class, however, didn't appear to have any good assignments from which to choose. Two assignments were to units which were listed as the 4628th and 4629th SS. When I asked the enlisted man who was handling the assignments what those organizations were, he said he didn't know, but he thought they were supply squadrons in California. And I thought, boy, that's not for me. The lowest-standing men in our class were stuck with assignments in these SS units, supply squadrons, we thought. Actually, they were special squadrons set up to check people out in jet aircraft. Because nobody knew what these units were, the men with the lowest standing in our class ended up flying jets.

When I looked over the list of assignments available, the only interesting assignment I could see was flying T-6s at Hensley Field, near Dallas, Texas. At least it was a flying position; some assignments were non-flying positions. I selected Hensley Field, and I flew as an instructor for the Air Force Reserves for about a year and a half, instructing in T-6s, T-11s, C-47s, and C-46s. While I was at Hensley Field, I was assigned as an assistant operations officer and the Reserve Records Administrator, with an additional duty as assistant to the flight surgeon. I think I was given that job because my family members frequently suffered from various illnesses and I came to know the flight surgeon well. I was also given the job of assistant Officer's Club officer and assistant Base Marshal, and if any other job came up I was usually assigned that too. We'd work all week at the base, and on the weekends we would fly to various airfields around Texas where we would let the reservists fly the airplanes to maintain proficiency. Each Friday we'd fly the airplanes out to different locations around the state of Texas. We'd give the reserve officers who showed up a quick check ride and tell them "away you go." They would fly the airplanes around for a couple of days, practicing their flying proficiency. After they finished their training, we'd get in the planes on a Sunday night and fly back to Hensley Field.

At Hensley I was assigned the job of checking a former B-17 pilot out in the T-6. I was in the back seat of the airplane while he flew the airplane from the front seat. I'd already demonstrated how to land the airplane several times. Apparently he thought he was still flying a B-17, because he tried to land the airplane about ten feet in the air and stall it out. We lost airspeed and started falling towards the runway. I grabbed the stick and tried using my rudder pedals to "walk it down" in a stall to the runway—Kabang! We bounced hard on the runway, but we were all in one piece. After he did that, we thoroughly discussed the proper procedure for landing the T-6, which was, after all, an easier airplane to land than the B-17. The next time he came in to land, he tried the same thing, but this time he kicked full rudder in. I have no idea why he did that, but a full rudder in a stall condition puts the airplane in a spin. And when you're only about ten to fifteen feet above the ground, entering into a spin is NOT the thing to do. I had to overpower his full rudder and try to keep that T-6 from starting to stall and spin. I said, "I'm not flying with you ever again." I don't remember whatever happened to that man, but he darn near killed me—I remember that.

While we were there, my oldest son, Cecil Jr., developed a physical problem. He began dragging his leg while he was walking. We took him to the flight surgeon, who came to our house to do a spinal tap on him and my second son, Bryan, and my wife. The next thing I knew he gave us a call and took us into a Dallas hospital—Cecil, Jr., had polio. Bryan and Margaret did not have polio, although they had some of the symptoms. After treatment, Cecil, Jr., recovered but residual problems developed later, including some spinal deformity, foot problems requiring a triple arthrode-sis operation, some hip abnormality, and uneven leg length. While we were at Hensley Field our children had a number of other childhood illnesses, including measles, mumps, and chicken pox.

We bought a new house while we were there. It was my first oppor-tunity to buy a home. But I should have remembered what happens when you buy a new home—you receive orders to move. Sure enough, I received orders assigning me to Alaska. To make it worse, I was assigned not as a pilot, but as a radar observer. I took my family to San Antonio, to my wife's parents' home, to stay there until I could find a place for them in Alaska. It was not an accompanied tour, so if we did bring our dependents, we had to pay for travel costs ourselves. After placing my family in San Antonio, I traveled to San Francisco and checked in for overseas processing. Alaska, not then a state, was considered an overseas assignment at that time. I trav-eled by train to Malmstrom Air Force Base, near Great Falls, Montana, and from there I caught a flight to Anchorage, Alaska.

After I reached Alaska, in July of 1949, I called my wife and told her to bring the children up so that we could be together. She piled the chil-dren into our car and drove up to Seattle, where she had the car shipped up to Alaska. She and the children flew up on a commercial plane from Seattle to Anchorage. In the meantime I had been using my off-duty time to find a place for my family. Anchorage was a small town in those days and there were few places to rent. The only place I could find was a build-ing resembling a two-car garage that had been converted into living quar-ters. There was a building less than one hundred yards from us that was never open during the day. It was called the Green Lantern. I had no idea what it was—we never saw any normal activity there. It opened after dark; it was a place where male patrons came in and had their off-duty activities, drinking and partying. It was rumored that ladies of easy virtue were pres-ent there as well. We moved to another location in a hurry.

When I reported in to the personnel office of the Alaskan Air Com-mand, they told me they had the perfect assignment for me. They wanted me to be the adjutant of a B-17 squadron. The position called for a rated navigator, which I had been before I became a pilot. They told me that I could be assigned there as a navigator, do my work as an adjutant, but I could fly as a copilot, and maybe check out on a B-17. According to them, it was a great deal all the way around. But I said, no, I was a pilot, and not only was I a pilot, I had jet time. There were three jet squadrons assigned to the base, and I wanted to get into one of the squadrons, which were all flying the P-80. This argument continued for a week or two, until the personnel people finally gave in and agreed to assign me to the 66th Fighter Squadron.

I reported to the 66th Fighter Squadron to check out in the P-80. During the acrobatic portion of one of my initial flights, I experienced an unexpected engine flameout. I restarted the engine and came back and landed. That experience was quite exciting, because I had never experienced an unintentional flameout in the air before. It gets very quiet in the cockpit when the engine quits. On another flight, I was doing some acrobatic maneuvers when I pulled excessive back pressure on the control stick and blacked out. I was in the bottom of a loop and pulled back on the stick with too much force for too long a period of time. I estimated that I pulled so much back pressure that my body felt as if it weighed nine times as much as it did normally, experiencing nine "Gs," as we called it. I pulled this excessive back pressure for several seconds, with the result that all the blood drained from I head and I blacked out. When I came to, I was going straight up in the air. My vision slowly returned; the first thing I noticed was a strange checkered pattern in my vision. Then I noticed that my arms and legs were shaking uncontrollably, as if I had a severe case of palsy. I was able to regain control of the aircraft before it stalled. I rolled the aircraft over and then leveled out, while I made sure my body was going to function normally again. This was a frightening incident, as I had never blacked out in my life.

The week after I was assigned to the squadron, an order issued by the Office of the Secretary of Defense announced that there was going to be a reduction in force. Two officers from each fighter squadron had to be identified for release, and each squadron had to meet the quota. Major Popovich, my squadron commander, was contacted and selected the names of two individuals in the squadron for release from the Air Force; mine, as I eventually discovered, was one of them. Because I was the newest man in the squadron, and the least experienced, and probably the least productive, my name was submitted. But I was never informed that my name had been submitted.

I continued in my training program in the squadron until November 1949, when I was called into the squadron commander's office and told to report to the fighter wing headquarters personnel office. When I did, I saw five other men there, two from each of the other squadrons and another individual from my squadron. They were laughing and swearing, and when they saw me they said, "Oh, you got it too." And I said, "Got what? What are you talking about?" And they said, "Don't you know why you're here? We're all being separated from the service. There's a reduction in force." This was how I found out I was leaving the squadron and the U. S. Air Force.

I departed Elmendorf Air Force Base in late November. My wife and sons waited a few days at the base and then were flown down to Great Falls, Montana. I drove my car, a 1948 Packard, down the Alcan Highway. It took me six or seven days to drive the Alcan. On a curve at the bottom of one of the hills, I hit a patch of ice, slipped off the road, hit the side of the mountain, bounced across the road, and went into a small ditch. The ditch was only eighteen inches deep, but it kept me from going over the side of a 2000-foot drop. But as a result, my right front wheel was bent in about 20 degrees—the whole axle was badly bent. So I drove the rest of the way on one side of my right front tire. I had to keep rotating tires, as the bad wheel rapidly wore the tire out on one side. Every place I stopped, I asked if someone had the capability of fixing my axle, but no one was able to repair it until I arrived in Great Falls.

At Great Falls I picked up my family and we drove to Selfridge Field, Michigan. I placed my wife and children with my parents until I was officially discharged from the Air Force. I found a job in Michigan with the Zilwaukee Gas and Storage Company, a company that pumped natural gas that had been piped up from the fields in the Texas panhandle to underground storage in tanks in Michigan. I didn't really care for that kind of work; it wasn't too long before my wife and I decided we didn't want to stay in Michigan any longer, and we packed up and drove down to San Antonio. In San Antonio I worked for the Franklin Life Insurance Company as an agent, but I soon found out I wasn't cut out to be a life insurance agent either. In the meantime, my wife was pregnant, and our third son, Rodney, was born in San Antonio's Nix Hospital on the 30th of April, 1951. We had another mouth to feed and I wasn't sure what kind of job I could find that would satisfy me.

Then one day I read an advertisement in the local paper, which indicated that the Air Force needed navigators, radar observer bombardiers, and jet pilots. The Korean War had started a few months earlier, and the Air Force was looking for people with special skills. I had every one of the skills they said they needed, and so I thought to myself, it's time to go back in the Air Force.

CHAPTER 4

Checking Out
in the F-86 "Saberjet"

THE "POLICE ACTION" in Korea had turned into a shooting war, and I wanted to be involved. But as usual, the road that led to my return to the Air Force was not an easy one. First I called up the personnel office at 14th Air Force to volunteer; the person who answered said they would send me some forms to fill out. I waited, but no forms arrived. After about three weeks I called again. This time they said they didn't have any records showing my previous service, and they asked me to send copies of my records. Fortunately, I had made duplicate copies of my records when I left the Air Force, and I mailed them in. I also asked them to send me a form so I could apply for extended active duty, because I was on inactive reserve status. Finally the form arrived. I filled it out and sent it back. Two or three weeks later I received a reply which said, we received your application, thank you very much, but we don't have any need for you at this time, and we'll keep your form on file.

Every week the newspapers contained advertisements saying the Air Force needed rated personnel with Air Force Specialty Codes (AFSCs) of 0142, 1059, and 1034. I had every one of these AFSCs. In frustration, I called the personnel office again, saying the Air Force needed specially qualified people, and that I was qualified. "We don't know anything about those ads," they said; "we'll let you know if we need you."

Well, I thought, I'll try another route. The Army needed pilots to fly in small airplanes as forward air controllers. I went to the Army recruiters and described my flying experience, and they said they would love to have me fly airplanes for them. I signed their forms, filled out the paperwork necessary for resigning my Air Force commission, and went home to wait for developments.

First I received a notice from the Air Force saying that my resignation had been accepted, unless I was recalled to active duty before I was sworn in as a member of the Army reserve corps. Three days before I was scheduled to be sworn in to the United States Army Aviation Department with a reserve commission as a first lieutenant, I received a message from Western Union at seven o'clock in the morning. The message said, by direction of the President, you are hereby directed to report to Brooks Air Base for a physical examination. Upon successful completion, you will receive further orders. I went to Brooks, took my physical, which I passed, and went home to wait. I notified the Army personnel office of the developments and they were very upset, not so much with me but with the Air Force.

I received orders shortly thereafter giving me a date to report to temporary duty, not as a pilot, but as a radar navigator bombardier at Mather Air Force Base in California. I decided I was not going to argue with the system at this point. I figured that once I was back in the Air Force it would be easier to sort out the confusion. When I arrived at Mather, I was told there were too many students in the entering class, and they were looking for volunteers to wait for the next class. Once again I was experiencing a delay in training, but this delay suited my plans perfectly. I immediately volunteered to wait for the next class, which started two weeks later. I used those two weeks to fly B-25s, especially to build up my instrument time. I flew as copilot and first pilot every day that I could. I accomplished every requalifying event except my instrument check, and I couldn't do that because I was on temporary duty status. But I completed all my other flying requirements to make me current for my instrument flying card. While this training was going on, my wife and children joined me, and we lived in Sacramento.

After I completed radar observer bombardier refresher training, my family and I returned to Randolph Air Force Base. When I arrived at Randolph and reported in, the operations people asked me what I was doing there. I told them that I had been incorrectly assigned, and that I should be flying as a pilot, not a navigator. I explained that my most recent rating was as a jet pilot, and the officer I talked to agreed that I was incorrectly assigned. He sent a telegram to Washington stating that my last aeronautical rating was as a pilot, I had been flying as a pilot, and I should be assigned as a pilot rather than as a navigator or a radar navigator-bombardier. It took about six weeks to get the results back from Washington, but to my surprise, Headquarters concurred. I was sent to Williams Field for jet refresher training and to become recurrent in the F-80 aircraft. After I completed training there, I would be assigned to Nellis Air Force Base for training in F-80s for further assignment to Korea. This news pleased me very much.

When I arrived at Williams Field, I was told that according to Air Force regulations I shouldn't have been sent there because I didn't have a current instrument card. For the next three weeks, operations people at Williams Field, Headquarters Air Force, and Headquarters Training Command argued about what they were going to do with me because I had shown up without an instrument card. Finally someone at the Pentagon made a decision: "Give him an instrument check," they said; "check him out, and send him on to Nellis." So they gave me an instrument check in a T-6, gave me my refresher training in the F-80, and sent me to Nellis.

We arrived at Nellis late in the afternoon. I went into Headquarters to sign in while my family waited outside in the car. Every afternoon at five o'clock an aircraft performed a "flagpole check"; each unit on the base competed to see who could be the most accurate, to fly directly over the flagpole exactly at 1700 hours—to the second. Each working day a jet would climb up to an altitude over the base, and then at the proper time it would make a pass down the field over the flagpole, which happened to be located at base headquarters, where my family was waiting in the car. When that jet came over at near-supersonic speed, maximum speed for that F-86, it practically lifted everyone right out of the car. It scared them to death. My wife, Margaret, thought the aircraft was going to crash—she just didn't know what was going on. When the jet passed overhead, I was waiting inside, hoping to start my in-processing. But when the aircraft roared by overhead, the clerk said, "It's five o'clock. The office is closed. Come back tomorrow." When I went outside, my family was still shaking.

I was given another checkout in a T-33 and then began F-80 ground school. After completing questionnaires on F-80 engineering and emergency procedures, I began flight instruction. At Nellis we received air-to-air engagement practice as well as some air-to-ground practice in weapons delivery. But we spent much of our time working on formation flying. About a month before I was scheduled to complete the F-80 program, we were told that about one-third of us were going to be checked out in F-86s, and I was one of those selected to transition into the F-86. When I learned I was going to be flying the F-86, I ran out and looked at that airplane, I was so excited. I don't know anything to compare it to—the top jet aircraft in the Air Force, and I was going to get to fly it. We were reassigned to F-86s because additional squadrons of F-86s were needed in Korea. The 51st Fighter Wing had been flying F-80s in Korea and had converted to F-86s in January of

1952, about six months before I went through jet training at Nellis. Many of the pilots in the 51st had completed their tour of duty in Korea, and a significant number of replacement pilots were needed.

When we checked out in the F-86, we first flew a few engineering familiarization flights, learning how the aircraft systems worked. Maneuvers in this phase included high-speed stalls and simulated forced landing patterns, and slow flight and turns at high altitude, to discover how sensitive the aircraft controls were at the high altitudes—40, 000 feet and above—at which the aircraft flew. We flew cross-country missions to observe the aircraft's typical range and fuel consumption rate. In our formation flights, we flew in two-ship and four-ship groups, in elements and flights, in fingertip formation. Later we learned to fly combat formation procedures, in which we flew in a spread formation to give us greater opportunity to observe the airspace around us. We learned also that high altitude flight required us to be spread out at a greater distance in turns due to the excessive amount of space that was needed to execute a turn.

After we completed formation flying, we practiced air-to-air combat, during which we fired at a sleeve towed by a target aircraft, usually a twin-engine A-26. The target was a nylon banner at which we made live firing passes. We had to be careful not to fire at the target from a position behind the tow aircraft, because our bullets might hit it. One of the unique design features on the F-86A aircraft was that it had leading edge slats that extended for takeoff and landing. Once airborne, we would lock the slats in the retracted position. But when we set up for a firing run on the target, it was easy to forget that the slats would not extend unless we unlocked them. We would leave what we called our "high perch" position, above and to the side of the target, roll into a dive, pick up speed, decrease our descent and turn right toward the target, and concentrate on picking up the correct picture in our gunsight. But if we weren't careful and forgot what would happen without slats extended, we would pull too many Gs and snap into a high-speed stall, and the aircraft would spin out of the run and we would have to recover. This happened to just about everyone at one time or another on our run-ins to the target, including me. After we flew the pattern a few times, we learned to identify the characteristics of an impending high-speed stall, and if we felt them, we did not fire but went through the firing run dry.

The method by which we scored our air-to-air hits was simple. After our flight finished its firing runs, we came back and landed, and the tow aircraft brought the sleeve back and dropped it over the field. We then examined the sleeve, counting the number of holes and recording the color of the holes. Each aircraft that was flying had different color paint coating the bullets it fired—red, yellow, green, blue—and the paint would adhere to the sleeve as the bullet passed through. We could determine the number of bullets we had fired from the aircraft, so determining the overall score was just a matter of figuring the number of hits compared to the number of bullets fired. We fired only two of our six .50 caliber guns, which were located in the nose of the aircraft, for otherwise we would have used up a lot of ammunition and shredded the tow target. I was not the best shot in the class nor was I the worst. I was about average. I recall that we flew about ten air-to air missions. We had limited time in the aircraft, so I did not feel too badly about the fact that my scores were not higher. After we completed the required number of air-to-air missions, we then practiced our air-to-ground missions. We flew a limited number of air-to-ground missions, however, because the F-86 was designed primarily for air-to-air missions.

I completed my training in the F-86 in May 1952. When I left Nellis I had about 35 total hours of flying time in the F-86. I installed my family in Michigan to live while I was in Korea. I flew from Chicago to San Francisco, caught a ride to Travis Air Force Base, California. We flew from Travis to Hawaii to Wake Island to Johnson Field, outside of Tokyo. My total jet flying time was 126 hours when I arrived at Johnson Field, which included 36 flights in the F-86.

CHAPTER 5

Initial Combat Experiences

I WAS ASSIGNED TO the 16th Fighter Squadron based at Suwon, Korea. We referred to the base as K-13. We were sent by train to an air base at Kisarazu, where we boarded another transport and flew to Korea. I arrived there on 30 May and was interviewed by Colonel Francis Gabreski, the great World War II ace. Colonel Gabreski invited all of us new arrivals in to talk to him. He said, "Well now, fellows, we don't have any problem getting pilots, so it's not a big deal if you don't want to fly combat; we can take care of that. So if any of you don't want to, just let me know and we'll find you another assignment." Of the five of us who listened to Colonel Gabreski, none of us volunteered to get out of combat. That was the only interview I ever had with Colonel Gabreski, who returned to the States about three or four weeks after I arrived. Those of us who had just arrived were sent back to Japan for a week of additional engineering training in the F-86. I reported in to the 16th Squadron around the middle of June.

For the first few days I spent a good deal of time sitting on alert in the cockpit of my F-86A. It was quite warm in late June, especially with the equipment I was wearing and carrying: flying suit, high-top boots, g-suit, inflatable life vest (which we called the "Mae West" for obvious reasons), parachute, dingy and radio, and escape kit. On one mission I flew as a spare heading into North Korea for the first time. But because I wasn't needed, I was released to return to K-13, and as I headed south I had a chance to see the ships off the west coast, anchored in the Inchon harbor—aircraft carriers, light and heavy cruisers, and many landing craft. Any time we flew a scheduled mission into the airspace over North Korea, we were given credit for a combat mission, regardless of whether or not we engaged

29

Formation of F-86 aircraft of 51st Fighter Wing over Korea, 1952.

with enemy aircraft. I was able to fly four combat missions in the month of June, followed by fifteen missions in July.

By the middle of July I had flown thirteen missions but had been involved in little combat activity myself. On the 12th of July we ran into several MiGs which circled in behind us as we were turning. The number two man in the flight took some hits and had to bail out. As the number four man, I was busy protecting my element leader while he shot at the MiGs. I saw then that the MiG was an excellent airplane, as it pulled away from us in a climb as we were chasing them in full throttle. By the end of July I had completed 19 missions and was becoming familiar with what was expected of a pilot flying the wing of a lead aircraft. I was assigned to D flight; my flight commander was Captain James E. Tilton, who was, for some unusual reason, on temporary duty to Korea from England. My first combat missions were quite uneventful. We took off and flew combat air patrols up and down the Yalu River. When I first arrived at K-13, there were no restrictions about flying across the border, so everybody was tasked to go up and down the Yalu. In some cases we were tasked to go up to Antung, on the other side of the Yalu, and see if any aircraft were taking off or flying in the area.

On my twentieth mission, I experienced my first close encounter with a MiG. I was flying number two in a flight of four. We were about three-quarters of the way to the Yalu River when one of our pilots lost his engine and headed back towards Cho-do Island. He couldn't restart his engine, and he had to bail out over the island. Fortunately, he was immediately picked up by air-sea rescue. Once we knew he was safe, my flight leader and I turned north again to patrol along the Yalu. On my next mission, we were flying combat air patrol at 35,000 feet when he spotted an aircraft down low—right off the ground. We put the speed brakes out, went to idle, and headed straight down. As we approached the ground, we pulled the speed brakes in, put the power back on, and headed toward what we now could see were two MiGs. The MiG on the right hand side had his gear down and the one on the left hand side was flying almost line abreast, watching him. They were fairly close to the ground. The flight leader took the one on the right with his gear down, and I kept clearing him as required. I lined up on the other MiG, on the left wing, who was even with the one with the gear down. As we got within 2000 feet, I kept clearing Jim; "You're clear," I'd say. "Roger," he'd say, whenever I called. But he never cleared me to fire on the other MiG.

For whatever reason, this MiG was apparently making an emergency landing in a rice paddy, and the other MiG flying on his wing at a slow speed was watching the first MiG. Jim took a shot at the MiG that was making the deadstick landing into the rice paddy. I had my gunsight on the second MiG when Jim fired. His MiG continued straight ahead, and just as we passed over him, he hit the ground and cartwheeled. I had to make a little maneuver to get by the other MiG without ramming him; I just barely passed to the side as we went by. I wonder what that pilot thought we were doing and why he didn't get shot at. I had to go through without firing because I had not been cleared to fire by my flight leader. That was the rule: you did not shoot unless you had been cleared to shoot. We went straight through, and kept on going. After we passed over them, the anti-aircraft fire started coming up at us. The flak was really thick, but it was bursting behind us. We were going fast, about .95 or .96 Mach.

We climbed back up to altitude and stayed there until our fuel was too low to continue our mission. When we hit "bingo fuel" at 1200 pounds aboard the aircraft we headed for home. After we landed, I asked Jim, "Why didn't you clear me to shoot at the other MiG?" And he said, "I never thought of it; I was so intent on getting one MiG, it never dawned on me to clear you to shoot at the other MiG." I said, "I had him in my sights all the way." He said he was sorry but it had just not occurred to him. We'd have had two MiGs instead of one.

Major Dwight Beckham was our squadron commander at this time. He was an excellent leader with combat experience in the European Theater in World War II. I was able to fly on his wing a few times; some of those flights were quite memorable. On one mission, we were supposed to provide top cover for an RB-45 that was flying north, into Manchuria, to take some pictures. The weather was very bad, with lots of clouds, and when we flew to our rendezvous point, we were at 20,000 feet in the clouds. We orbited for a quite a while as we talked to our bomber, and the GCI controller tried to get us together. I was on Major Beckham's left wing, and the second element was on the right wing. We were flying fingertip formation in the weather so we could stay together. Suddenly, from the right, at about the 2:30 position, I spotted the B-45 coming straight at us but about 20 feet low. I don't know exactly how much distance separated us—it wasn't much—but it was too close, and at that 90 degree closing angle, we went whistling by each other almost on a collision course. If we would have been 20 to 30 feet lower, all aircraft—the B-45 and all of us—would have collided. I called out the B-45, but by the time I called him out, the bomber had already passed underneath us.

On another mission when I was flying on Major Beckham's wing, we were heading due north, towards the Yalu. We hadn't seen any contrails, we had heard no calls, we had heard nothing from GCI—we were just flying along in a combat spread formation. All of a sudden, just about the time we arrived at the Yalu, a MiG flew head-on between Major Beckham and me. It went screaming through us at a rate of closure nearing Mach 2. Our normal cruise speed was about .96 Mach, and the MiGs flew at comparable speeds. After I saw the one MiG, I saw many MiGs; all I could see were MiGs. I called out "MiGs!" I said, "MiGs! MiGs! MiGs!" I didn't even have a chance to say where they were, and the number four man started calling them out about the same time. We went right through them. I was clearing to the right and to the rear, and Major Beckham and the element leader were clearing across and in front of the flight. Somehow, they never saw these MiGs until we had passed through the MiG formation. There were somewhere between 80 and 100 MiGs and we went right through the middle of them. We made a 180 degree turn, but by the time we completed our turn, the MiGs were out of sight. They were gone. They didn't stay around for combat at all. They were gone.

When we got back on the ground, we talked it over to try to determine how many we saw, and why we hadn't seen them coming. It was really disturbing to suddenly see them and fly right through them, head on. One hundred MiGs! They must have had several groups of aircraft up there, and they must have been trying something new; they were all spread out, not in close formation. There were so many MiGs we just couldn't count them all. And we didn't get one. Nobody took a shot. Not one of us.

Later, on another mission, I was on Major Beckham's wing, heading home after an uneventful mission. We had seen nothing. We were about 20,000 feet, when all of a sudden I saw flak exploding just below our aircraft. I had never seen flak at altitude and I really didn't know what flak looked like. When I saw it I said, "Flak! Climb!" But Beckham came back, with his World War II experience, and said "Negative! Dive!" It was exploding underneath us, but by diving, we were able to gain speed and keep it behind us. If we had climbed, we would have slowed down and the flak would have burst right underneath us. We would have had a good chance of getting hit. This was another lesson I learned from an old head.

In August I flew ten more missions. Throughout the month many squadron pilots began rotating home, and someone made the decision that it was time to check me out as an element leader. For my checkout flight I was assigned to fly a mission as an element lead with an experienced pilot on my wing who watched how I flew the mission and handled my combat maneuvers. I guess I did all right, for I was approved to fly as an element leader. By the end of August I had 29 combat missions on my record and I was checked out as element lead. When September rolled around, I hadn't yet flown a combat mission, other than my checkout flight, as an element lead.

CHAPTER 6

My First Combat Victories in Korea

THERE HADN'T BEEN MUCH SUCCESS in the 51st Fighter Wing during this time. Every once in a while someone would tangle with a MIG, and the Wing would get credit for a kill, but very infrequently. We just weren't seeing that many enemy aircraft. On the seventh of September, however, I tangled with MiGs and had my first real combat experience as an element leader.

It was supposed to be my day off. I took my time shaving, showering, and brushing my teeth. Then I put on my uniform. The Air Force hadn't yet figured out what our official uniform would be. There was a blue wool outfit, experimental at the time, I believe, because the pants looked like knickers that extended below the knee. We wore long socks where the pants stopped. I was wearing a set of these. My flight was not scheduled for any activity, and after I had my breakfast, I grabbed my camera and hitched a ride down to the flight line. It was a beautiful day—clear sky, no clouds—and I thought I would go down to the flight line and watch the aircraft coming in to land to see if anybody came in with a dirty nose. If an aircraft landed with powder residue on either side of the intake, then I knew the pilot had had a chance to shoot at a MiG and I would go over and take a picture and find out what happened. It was always exciting to talk to someone who'd had a chance to shoot at a MiG. Our fighter wing was tasked to fly a maximum effort so there was a real possibility that someone would engage the enemy this day.

I walked into our squadron operations center. Captain Carl T. ("C.T.")

Weaver, our operations officer, was behind the ops counter. There were several other pilots in the ops area. Lieutenant Robert L. Sands, our A Flight Commander, was briefing two new people assigned to him. He was describing what combat was like and what our combat procedures were. The two new pilots had had their local checkout and they were learning what was going to happen on their next mission. That day our squadron had the responsibility to stand alert duty. Sometimes the squadron had the duty to fly combat missions, sometimes it had to provide the mobile control officer, and the tower officer, and sometimes it had to perform alert duty, where four aircraft would be on alert status, next to the runway. Four pilots would sit in or near these alert aircraft, waiting to fly if they had to. They would go out just before sunup and wait until about an hour and half had passed and then they would be through, unless they were tasked to provide standby alert for the scheduled combat missions.

Our squadron had alert duty that day. I was walking around in the operations area, shooting the breeze, and Lieutenant Sands was briefing the two newcomers, Captain Phil Hunting and Lieutenant Les Erickson. The field phone, which was our communications link to our group or wing headquarters, rang, and I heard C. T. Weaver respond that we had four aircraft in commission but only three pilots available to fly them. Lieutenant Sands' flight was up for alert duty, so he had three men ready, but no one was available to fly in the element lead, or number three, position. Weaver indicated that Wing wanted someone to sit on alert in the alert aircraft until the alert flight returned. The original alert flight had been launched earlier in the day. Sands said he had three other pilots available, but none had been checked out as an element lead.

I said, "I'm checked out as an element lead." Weaver looked at me for a moment and then said, "This is your day off. Let's see if we can't find someone else, someone who's scheduled to fly today." He asked a couple of other pilots who walked by if they could fill in, but they were new pilots, and neither of them was an element lead. Finally, Weaver said that since no one else was available, and Wing wanted us to get set up right away, it would be all right if I went out and sat in one of the aircraft as element lead. In the meantime, he said, he would try to find a qualified pilot who was supposed to be scheduled and send him out to replace me. "That's fine with me," I said, and started to walk out the door. As I did so, the phone rang again, and C. T. picked up the phone, then hollered, "Scramble!" which meant that our alert flight was supposed to take off immediately.

I ran over to our squadron operations building on the flight line, where our personal equipment room was located. I opened my locker, pulled out my flying clothes, and hurried out of my uniform. The other men were already in their flying gear, so all they had to do was grab their helmets and their parachutes and head for their airplanes. They were calling out airplane tail numbers as we went rushing out the door. I was still trying to change while the other men were running towards their airplanes. I could hear the auxiliary power units starting to fire up. I made the most rapid change of clothing I have ever made, and pretty soon I was on my way to my airplane, too.

Fortunately, my aircraft was close to the personal equipment building. As I was heading out, one of the other officers ran out with me, and as I got into the cockpit, he jumped onto the nose of my aircraft and straddled it. The crew chief helped me strap in, while another pilot ran around the aircraft performing the preflight. By the time I finished strapping in, the APU was going, and the captain who was straddling the nose of my aircraft was starting the engine for me. When I got my seat belt fastened and adjusted my seat, he had gotten the engine running. He slid off the side of the aircraft, gave me a thumbs up, and I started taxiing. I was the second aircraft to taxi. Sands was first, and I was right on his tail.

We hit the runway for a rolling takeoff, and I closed the canopy. Just as we got airborne, Sands called, "I've got to abort. I can't get my gear up." The F-86 had an emergency gear extension handle inside the cockpit that was often used by maintenance personnel when they performed maintenance work in the nose gear section. But it had to be reset before flight. If it had been used and not reset, the gear would not retract. That was what had happened with Sandy's aircraft. So he had to turn around and come back and land. The other two new pilots, Hunting and Erickson, had gotten airborne and were right behind me. We were heading north, and I was now the flight leader. I was heading into combat, leading two new pilots on their first real combat mission; they'd never been North before, and I had never seen them before this morning. I hadn't talked to them before, and at that time I didn't even know their names.

This was my 36th mission. It was an absolutely beautiful, clear day, a great day for flying. I checked the flight in on the combat radio frequency, where we were told we were going to provide air cover for the withdrawal of the main force of F-86 aircraft. They were up on a maximum effort mission, and most of the aircraft were starting to head back to base. The GCI controllers had noted that many aircraft were taking off from various airfields north of the Yalu River. Our aircraft were getting low on fuel and if they were to tangle with the MiGs now, many of them wouldn't be able to get home. The GCI site could see the MiGs forming up, and that was why we were scrambled and headed up their way.

We crossed the bomb line, tested and armed our six .50 caliber machine guns, and continued on our way. Our policy was that we did not go into combat as a single aircraft; two aircraft had to fly together. If we got split up, while in combat, we were supposed to depart immediately, heading for home. There needed to be at least two aircraft in a formation; ideally, four. In a three-aircraft formation, one aircraft would not have anybody clearing him. Our procedures called for any spare aircraft to divert to Cho-do Island, off the west coast of Korea, until there was no need for him. Then he would return to base. I sent Captain Hunting, who was supposed to be on Lieutenant Sands' wing, over to Cho-do Island. I told him to orbit there until we reached the Yalu River and if he wasn't needed then, he was released to return to K-13.

As Lieutenant Erickson and I continued north, we could see numerous contrails. The sky was full of them, like a mass of giant white worms crawling across the sky. There appeared to be hundreds of airplanes flying at the contrail level. When we approached the Yalu River area, I told Captain Hunting he was cleared to return to K-13. I could see contrails above and in front of me. As we flew closer, I could see that many of the contrails indicated that aircraft were in the process of joining into combat formations. We were at 38 or 39 thousand feet. Then I noticed eight MiGs at our 1130 position, just to the left of our nose, and just about level with us. They were flying two abreast, in elements, in trail, so there were two, two, two, and two. They began to turn left, and I turned inside their turn to cut them off.

We jettisoned our drop tanks and approached them from about their seven o'clock position, to their left rear. As we began to close, they began to increase their turn, and when I moved within about 2000 feet, and was getting ready to take a shot at one of them, Les Erickson said, "Lead, we've got eight more MiGs coming at us from six o'clock!"

The first MiG flight then tightened up their left climbing turn to evade us and forced us to the outside of their turn. The MiGs approaching us from our six o'clock position were getting in fairly close, so I set my sights on the number seven man of the first flight of eight, and got off a shot. Just as I did that, Les said "Break left!" and Les and I both broke left. The second flight had excess speed on us and that caused them to swing wide, and go beyond us to the outside. They went shooting by, off our right wing. I pulled my nose up and did a big, loose barrel roll to the right. I had to be careful, because at our altitude I couldn't do too much in the way of aerobatic maneuvers or I would stall out. My maneuver caused us to lose just enough airspeed that we fell back slightly and rolled out in the six o'clock position of the second flight of MiGs.

I was in a good position to fire, but I had to line up on the aircraft in front. I lined up again, and this time I took aim at the last element leader—he was closer to me—in this flight of eight in front of me—we had sixteen MiGs now. The first flight of eight had kept climbing and turning and they were now over at our nine o'clock position, off our left wing, and I was behind the second flight. Just as I was getting ready to shoot, Les called out again, "We've got eight MiGs coming in from six o'clock!" This was another flight of eight. And this flight was shooting at us. We were pretty busy looking around to see who was shooting at us and where everybody was.

These MiG pilots appeared to be very well trained and disciplined. They held their positions, even though we were coming in and lining up on them. Then I got a chance to take another shot. But the third group approaching us caused us to break off again. We broke left, level, and the third flight of MiGs that was on our tail pulled on up beyond us. They started slowing down but passed us to our right. We were flying in a left turn, with 24 MIGs and two F-86s in a giant Lufbery circle up around 38 or 39 thousand feet. We were all going round and round together.

Each time I fired, I lost airspeed and position, but Les Erickson cut in on the inside, and I said, "Okay, you take a shot." So then he would take a shot at them. And while he was doing that, I could lower my nose a little to gain airspeed, cut to the left, get a little to the inside of him, and as he lost position and airspeed as a result of shooting, I'd cut in front of him and take a shot. At 38,000 feet, it takes miles and miles to make an orbit. You have to be very easy on the controls—a feather touch—if you pull too many Gs, you're going to hit a high speed stall, lose airspeed and altitude and be at the mercy of the other guys.

These MiG pilots were willing to fight; they didn't stay up at a higher altitude, they were ready to come down and mix it up with us; they knew they had us outnumbered, I guess. At 24 to 2 odds, they must have thought they had the advantage. But I think we had an advantage, because any time I saw an airplane, if I could get in position, I could shoot at it and not have to worry whether it was one of ours or not. But they had to find the right two to shoot at. We had a pretty good opportunity to shoot at the MiGs. I don't know how many times I took a quick shot; I don't know how many times Les took a quick shot. One time I saw his bullets hit one of the aircraft, and one time he saw my bullets strike an aircraft. We shot several times at the same aircraft, because we were aiming at the "tail-end charlies" of each of the three flights of aircraft.

This maneuvering went on and on and on. We must have been in that Lufbery for almost 45 minutes. While we were playing cat and mouse with

24 MiGs, Erickson called out, "Did you switch sides?" I said, "No." I looked to my right and there was a MiG, coming up at my three o'clock position, perfectly level, not trying to get into a combat position on us. He looked like he was trying to join up on us. I have no idea what this pilot was doing, whether he was an instructor trying to lead someone into us, or whether he didn't recognize that we were not part of the MiG formation. I have no idea. I can only conjecture as to what he was trying to do. I don't think he was a defector. If he was, he picked a bad time to defect.

This MiG was sitting out there about a thousand feet to my right. As soon as I saw him, I instinctively did another large barrel roll over and came down behind him, about 1200 or 1500 feet behind him. I was losing speed, but I lined up on him and started shooting at him and I saw lots of hits on the airplane. Les and I had been shooting so often that we didn't know how much ammunition we had left. But I shot some long bursts into him and he just stayed in his position and let me shoot at him. He went straight ahead and I kept shooting. About this time, Les called "Here come eight more. Break left!"

This new flight of MiGs was about 1500 to 2000 feet behind us, and I saw them shooting at us. At the same time I saw that we were down to bingo fuel. I told Les to follow me, because we were low on fuel and it was definitely time to go home. We rolled hard left; as we did, the approaching flight shot on by. As they did I pulled my nose through and pointed it at the ground, did a modified split S, a steep dive out of an inverted position, and Les followed me. We rolled out somewhere between 25,000 feet and 20,000 feet and as we hit maximum speed I kept full power on and started climbing back to the south. When I looked back, I was relieved to see that nobody was following us.

We stayed in combat the whole time we were up there in what must have been one of the longest jet-to-jet combat engagements in the Korean War. We were pretty excited as we headed for home. After we landed we went into debriefing and each claimed a damaged aircraft. Within a week or ten days after our flight and unknown to me, Lieutenant Erickson was called into a war claims board meeting, and asked what he saw during the fight. On the 25th of September, my claim was upgraded from a damaged aircraft to a kill. To say that this combat was incredibly exhilarating would be an understatement. My adrenaline was pumping like an oil well in Oklahoma.

It was the first time I had ever shot at anything except a towed target in my life. The feeling you have when you see an enemy aircraft, put it in your sights, and pull the trigger is a feeling that cannot adequately be described. And to see somebody shooting at you, and to watch the bullets

Cecil Foster after shooting down his first MiG, September 1952.

come at you, in slow motion it seems, is also a feeling you cannot describe. It is something you have to experience to appreciate. When your six .50 caliber machine guns are all firing at the same time, the recoil causes your airplane to slow down noticeably. And the noise of the guns firing gives a terrific sense of power. Two weeks after my first successful engagement with the MiGs, I was appointed D Flight Commander of the 16th F.I.S. Captain Bart, the previous flight commander, was appointed as squadron assistant operations officer.

On September 26, my flight was scheduled to fly a combat air patrol (CAP) mission. Captain Bart was designated as the flight leader, and I was flying as an element leader with Second Lieutenant Al Grenz as my wingman. This was Al's first combat mission. Our take off, join up, gun check, and combat spread maneuvers were normal. We retained our drop tanks until combat was imminent.

We flew to the mouth of the Yalu and turned east northeast, just south of the river. We were flying at 35,000 feet with the sun at our back. There were no contrails in our vicinity, although we could see many farther north. Captain Bart then spotted two MiGs ahead of us, crossing from left to right and slightly below us. He called for us to drop our tanks and began a descending hard right turn towards the MiGs' stern position. His dive was forcing us out of a good protective situation, so I began a climbing left turn which I intended to follow with a rapid reversal to put us in position to cover the flight leader. As soon as I started my climb, I was surprised to see six pairs of white puffs of smoke, which I first called as "Flak!" and then realized the puffs were caused by MiGs dropping their fuel tanks, as we crossed through a formation of MiGs. I saw the MiGs flying in trail with each wingman close behind, and I made a hard reversal to the right.

The MiG flight leader was in a hard left turn, and we entered a scissors maneuver, cutting across each other's nose. The MiG leader fired at us, much too early. "Bad shot!" I thought. I rolled level and called Captain Bart, informing him that I was in a scissors maneuver with six MiGs and could use a little help. As I called, I fired a one-second burst with my six .50 caliber guns. I watched my tracers fly toward the MiG in what seemed like slow motion as I heard Captain Bart acknowledge my call for assistance. My tracers passed just aft of the lead MiG's tail, and my bullets subsequently stitched a row of hits along the fuselage of his wingman. At that same instant the lead MiG exploded in a large black and orange fireball. I yelled out over the radio, "The MiG exploded! And number two is burning!" The wingman's aircraft was emitting brown and black smoke as I pulled up sharply to miss the remaining MiGs as they flew past. If they fired at us, they didn't hit us.

I kept my eyes on the second MiG as it appeared to stop in the air and my nose climbed almost to vertical. I continued with a rolling pullover and entered a nearly vertical dive as I followed the crippled, inverted MiG. I fired a short burst and then realized I was about to have a mid-air collision with it! I rotated my aircraft a quarter turn counterclockwise as my right wing passed between the MiG's wing and fuselage. That scare aged me ten years. I executed an immediate pull up and hard turn back toward the damaged MiG. It was falling like a leaf, still inverted. I then saw the MiG pilot floating beneath his parachute and a long red streamer dropping nearby. Later I wondered why he had opened his parachute at 35,000 feet. Maybe he had forgotten to disconnect his low altitude ejection lanyard.

I called to my wingman, "Are you still with me?" I don't know how he did it, but he stayed with me. We then flew toward the pilot as I took pictures with my gun camera after placing my firing controls in the "safe" position. I didn't get a picture, however, because I passed too close, directly over the top of the parachute. The MiG pilot was frantically waving his arms.

He was either worried that I was going to shoot at him or was struggling to connect his oxygen bottle. I seriously doubt he survived the bailout.

In contrast to my mission on 7 September, this combat lasted only seconds. From the time I spotted the MiGs dropping their tanks until the time the second MiG was disabled, only about six seconds elapsed. When I looked at my gun camera film, I saw that when I nearly collided with the second MiG, it had lost its horizontal stabilizer, accounting for its lack of stability.

We eventually figured out why the first MiG exploded when I thought my burst had missed him. Prior to the mission the 51st had received several new F-86s. The aircraft I flew, aircraft number 868, had passed its acceptance check only the night before, but there was no time to boresight its guns. Tracers were placed in only two of the six guns. One of the guns without tracers in its ammunition was later found to be firing considerably to the left of the aim point. The bullets from this gun hit the lead MiG and caused it to explode. After the mission, I asked Lieutenant Grenz how in the world he was able to stay with me during my wild maneuvering. His reply was simple but logical: "There was no way you were going to leave me alone with those MiGs!"

On the very next mission, I came as close to getting myself killed as I did the entire time I was in Korea. I never looked at death so closely as I did then. I was at 35,000 feet patrolling the Yalu with one wingman— Major Lahmeyer. I spotted four MiGs down low heading back across the river. I thought to myself, with false confidence as it turned out, "Here is victory number four, and maybe, if I'm lucky, number five." I rolled over with full power on and headed straight down, accelerating quickly. I went through Mach clean, without a burble, and leveled out behind one at about 4,000 feet and then dropped lower, to 2500 feet. I was gaining on the number four MiG rapidly, and was just about to squeeze off my first burst when I saw his element leader break left. But the aircraft I was following stayed on his heading. I looked around and saw MiGs one and two pulling around towards me as number three, the MiG that had turned left, started to swing around behind me as well. They had left MiG number four, the one I was chasing, as bait to pull me into a trap. They were willing to risk his life to claim mine. But I thought it was a lousy trade, so I broke right, directly into the first two MiGs. The lead MiG fired across my nose but missed. The second MiG, however, maneuvered towards me and I found myself about 1000 feet from him looking right down his gun barrels as he blazed away at me.

It suddenly occurred to me that I was finished. Even with good luck, I was sure my plane would be shot up and I would have to bail out. But somehow, the MiG's shells never touched my plane—not one part of it. The bullets must have missed my left wing and lower fuselage by inches. Then we flashed past each other and I was heading south with full power, leaving the area as fast as I could go. I looked around, but the MiGs were not following. I called my wingman to see if he was still with me. He replied that he was all right but that he had lost me. That was why I never heard a call warning me about the trap. If he had been with me he would have been able to see what the other MiGs were doing while I was chasing my MiG. Eventually we rejoined and I headed for home. I decided that I didn't need to worry about running up my score too quickly.

CHAPTER 7

Squadron Life in Korea

T HE LIVING QUARTERS for our pilots were located some distance away from our flight line buildings. There were two buildings per squadron; each long, rectangular building housed the men who made up two flights. There were three squadrons in the 51st Wing, so six of these buildings were required to house the pilots. In my flight quarters, we had little in the way of furniture. We found some wooden boxes which, with a little carpentering, we turned into shelves. I placed a piece of hard plastic sheeting on the wall on which I wrote the names of the flight members and the tasks we had to perform. Some of our duties included serving as the duty officer, the tower officer, mobile control officer, or flying "stovepipe," which was an early morning weather flight into the patrol area. We also scheduled a "spare," an extra pilot ready to fill in for someone else on short notice. We kept track of pilots who were away on temporary duty (TDY), or on rest and relaxation (R&R), or on duty not to include flying (DNIF). We also kept track of the number of missions that each pilot had flown to be equitable in scheduling our flights.

The flight commander in the other half of our building was Captain Charles Gabriel. He later became a four-star general and was chief of staff of the United States Air Force. Our flight had some pretty notable people in it. In my flight, D Flight, "Buzz" Aldrin was a member, joining just before I left the unit. Aldrin later became an astronaut. Just before I left, a new second lieutenant named McMillan arrived. He later became a three-star general. One of my wingmen, Lieutenant Ed Hepner, later became an assistant chief pilot for the Boeing Company.

The latrine facilities were located in a separate building, which we walked to on a boardwalk, an elevated board sidewalk, which helped to keep

44

the mud off our shoes. The showers and toilet facilities were located there. One of the most unusual features of the latrine was the automatic flush operation in the toilet. There was a row of seats cut out of a big plank—I think it was a ten-holer facility. A large tank of water was located at one end, which slowly filled with water. When it filled, an internal float tripped a valve and the water came rushing out, down the full length of the toilet facility, and by that means flushed the toilet.

Men who had been in the squadron for any length of time knew not to sit at the last hole, because when the water reached the far end, where the last hole was located, the water struck a baffle and splashed upwards, thoroughly wetting whoever happened to be occupying the last hole. If we saw someone sitting on that last hole, we knew he was new in the area. There was a heated shower at the other end of the latrine, and it was in heavy demand most of the time, especially in winter. Along the flight line were standpipes, four-inch metal pipes, driven into the ground, which we used to relieve our bladders when we weren't near a latrine. These were located at other places around the area as well. They were right out in the open, with no protective cover. But there were no ladies around, so we didn't have to worry about social modesty.

As a result of flying jets at high altitude, we discovered that certain foods were not good to eat if we were going to fly at high altitude. These foods included cucumbers, onions, and cabbage. It seemed to me that every day we had cucumbers and onions sliced in vinegar. That was our standard fare for salad. If we were served meat, it was generally hot dogs. Hot dogs don't work too well at high altitude either. I've never been especially fond of hot dogs since. Our mashed potatoes came out of a can—reconstituted potatoes. We had dried eggs for breakfast—again, reconstituted. These had a distinct flavor and looked like scrambled eggs but weren't. Every once in a while we had bacon. The bread was pretty good because it was baked locally, and we usually had butter to spread on it. The other meals were pretty nondescript.

A little later in my tour one of the other fighter squadrons, the 39th Fighter Squadron, started to fly F-86F models. These aircraft had bigger engines, longer wings, could go to higher altitudes, and could fly faster than the F-86E, which I was flying. When they received the F-86F, the men of the 39th were given a separate menu of food. This was part of an experiment to determine whether, if the men were fed more wholesome food, they would be more successful in combat. At the end of the dining area there was an elevated six-inch platform and the only people who could eat in this area were the pilots of the 39th Fighter Squadron. These men were given great food—steak, ice cream, cake. But the rest of us ate regular chow;

we weren't allowed to sample any of the food that was given to the men in the 39th Fighter Squadron. We were not happy about the situation.

Eventually I was selected as a wing combat training officer. I guess someone at a higher level must have thought I did a good job in flying formation. I was also thorough in explaining to new pilots how we flew our combat missions. As part of my training job I was tasked to brief the new pilots on our procedures in the combat zone, and show them how to fly the combat positions they would be expected to fly. I checked them out, flew with them on their first combat mission, and then turned them loose to the squadrons where they were assigned to a particular flight. But all of these activities were secondary to the main task of hunting MiGs.

Even though the MiG 15s were faster and could fly higher than the F-86, our guns were effective against the MiGs. We used the A1CM radar calibrating gunsight in the F-86E, which I had learned about at Nellis. I understood its operation reasonably well as a result of my training as a radar-navigator-bombardier. The radar-ranging gunsight computed firing indications based on range and movement data provided by radar and other cockpit instruments. When the radar locked on to an enemy aircraft, the reticle presented an image that increased in size as we approached the target aircraft. The farther away the target was, the smaller the reticle became. The system would lock on to an aircraft at any distance out to about 6000 feet. It computed the deflection angle according to the movement of the aircraft and the G forces on the aircraft, and placed the floating gunsight in the appropriate position. When the image of the enemy aircraft appeared in the reticle, all relevant factors had been taken into consideration, and when we pulled the trigger, our bullets should strike the target, regardless of range, airspeed, or altitude. Everything was calculated for the pilot. It was an excellent gunsight when it was working.

Many pilots didn't understand or didn't trust the gunsight. They thought it was inoperative sometimes, because it appeared to be pointing way off from the target as a result of the maneuvering of the target aircraft and their aircraft. Sometimes it appeared to be floating around, moving, because it was adjusting to the movements and forces of the two aircraft. So the pilots would put the sight in a fixed position and fly in close and shoot at the enemy with it in a fixed position. In that situation they would have to estimate their own lead angle and G-forces. Many of the pilots flew close to the enemy aircraft before they shot to ensure that they would hit their targets. But it wasn't necessary. I found that by using my gunsight I could hit the MiGs at distances as great as 3000 feet and be very effective.

When all six guns were firing on the F-86, the recoil action slowed the aircraft noticeably—it lost airspeed immediately. This loss of airspeed affected our ability to maneuver at high altitude, because we were already flying close to a stalled condition at our service ceiling. When we pulled the trigger, the aircraft immediately lost speed and could enter a high speed stall, unless we lowered the nose and regained airspeed. This was one of the tricks we had to learn when we were flying our combat missions. The six .50 caliber machine guns constituted an excellent weapon system, highly reliable, and absolutely ferocious to use against another aircraft. We could literally saw an aircraft in half if we could hold it in our sights long enough to fire at a range of 1000 to 1200 feet—the distance at which our gunsights were calibrated to converge their fire. If we hit an aircraft at that range with all six guns, it could be absolutely lethal.

CHAPTER 8

Almost an Ace

JUNE, JULY, AND AUGUST had not been particularly productive months for the wing, in terms of aircraft shot down. The MiGs were flying, but they were staying north of the Yalu River. Until August, everybody from the top commander down considered that it was allowable to go looking for MiGs where we could find them, even if that meant going across the Yalu. On the 22nd of August we received the word that we were no longer to fly across the Yalu River. We were told that if we crossed the border, we would be subject to disciplinary actions, including a court-martial. When that word came down, most pilots did not go across the border. We stayed on our side, and there just weren't very many MiGs coming up to challenge us. From that time on, nobody I knew crossed the Yalu to shoot down enemy aircraft. Much later, in January of 1953, I discovered that some of the pilots in the 4th and 51st Fighter Wings had continued to fly across the Yalu.

The month of September was a good month for me, for I flew 24 combat missions, six training missions, and some functional check flights. Check flights had to be flown on aircraft that had undergone maintenance and needed to be test flown before being placed on combat-ready status. On the 17th of September, I was promoted to flight commander and assumed command of D flight. I had been qualified as an element leader for only about two or three weeks when I was promoted to flight commander. This was a new experience and a new responsibility for me—I had never been a flight commander before, and had limited flying experience, so I had a lot to learn. Because I was the junior flight commander, whenever headquarters personnel wanted to log a combat mission, they assigned me as element leader while they flew the flight leader position.

September was a beautiful month for flying—a pilot's dream. We had many cool, clear days. There were almost no clouds. It was perfect for flying combat. The cold, clear days brought the contrail level down so that we could fly just underneath it. That contrail layer gave us protection from anyone flying above us. Any aircraft coming down from above would create contrails—moisture produced from the jet engine exhaust—and we'd be able to pick them up visually so they couldn't sneak in on us unseen. We used that phenomenon to good advantage. The MiGs always had an altitude advantage on us, so if we stayed just below the contrails, they couldn't see us and had to be vectored in towards us by their radar, but we could see them when they were at higher altitudes dropping down to attack. If they were above the contrail level, which happened occasionally, it didn't make much difference, because they had to drop down through the contrail level to engage us. We were always looking up against a blue sky, and when we saw an aircraft up there we were almost certain it was a MiG, because our service ceiling was not as high as that of the MiGs.

Often, when we engaged in combat, the element leader would become separated from the flight leader, especially when we started to engage with a number of MiGs. Then we would divide into elements of two, and the element leader and his wingman would operate as if they were an individual flight. They would cover one another and protect one another while maneuvering. When we flew into the enemy airspace, we almost always flew close to our maximum altitude, the service ceiling of the aircraft, depending on the height of the contrail level. We flew at a high airspeed, not quite at 100% power, until someone spotted an enemy aircraft. Once we engaged in combat, we put our throttles in maximum thrust position and left them in maximum thrust position until we disengaged from a combat situation. When flying at maximum throttle position, we flew our aircraft to maintain our desired position in the flight. If we were getting ahead of our position in the flight, we would gain altitude, which would cause us to lose airspeed, and then we would let our aircraft settle back into position. If we were falling back in position, we would dive our aircraft a little, pick up a little airspeed and then pull our nose up and climb back into position. We flew our aircraft in a manner so that we all could fly at maximum throttle position. Every time the flight leader changed heading, we were required to adjust appropriately for the change in position.

In our combat formations, the flight leader and the element leader were in the two attack positions, and the two wingmen served primarily as defensive men, keeping an eye out for other aircraft. In my flight, I established the rule that whoever spotted a MiG called it out. If either the flight leader or the element leader did not have the MiG in sight immediately, the wingman who spotted the aircraft would immediately initiate the maneuver required for the situation, whether it would be a bounce or a break. If it was a break, normally the wingman would call "Break left," with our call sign, or break right or break up or break down, whatever direction seemed appropriate, and we would instantly react. There was no time to question the command. Later, after the threat had passed, we would sort it out. Either the flight leader or element leader could initiate combat and be covered by the other element.

As D Flight commander, I checked everyone in the flight out as a flight leader and element leader, so that wherever we were or whenever we had to go on a mission, we would have enough pilots to fill in any flight with whatever position the mission required. Knowing the duties and challenges of the other positions in the flight, the men could function much more cohesively as a unit when we went up to fly. Everyone knew what the other man was going to do, and we melded into a family of pilots so that little thinking was required; everyone reacted instinctively.

Our normal procedure, when we took off from K-13, was to form in two-ship formations initially, and then the element lead, with his number two man, would join on the lead and his number two man, and we would fly fingertip four formation as we climbed out. We flew in a loose fingertip formation, and every one checked his aircraft, to make sure the arming switches were in the proper positions. After we crossed the demarcation line, the 38th parallel, we armed our weapons and test fired them to make sure they were all working. After we crossed the 38th parallel, we moved to our combat spread formation, which put the element lead almost in a line abreast position, parallel with the flight leader. The two wingmen would fall back slightly. This gave us the maximum defensive ability to spot other aircraft in the area and to clear each other. Each wingman cleared from his three o'clock position to his nine o'clock position, high and low to the rear. The flight leader and element leader scanned the three o'clock to the nine o'clock position in the forward area.

The month of October continued to provide good flying weather. It wasn't quite as good as September; the weather was getting colder, we had a few snowstorms, we had rain, sleet, the kind of weather to be experienced in Michigan or Ohio as the fall starts to turn into winter. We experienced more weather days and more days in which intermediate level clouds restricted our flight operations. We took off and flew through the clouds to the contrail level, placing ourselves just below it for defensive purposes.

On the 16th of October, eleven missions after I shot down the two MiGs with one gun burst, I was scheduled to lead a flight along the Yalu, on a combat air patrol near the Sui-ho Dam. The mission was nothing out of the ordinary and I had no reason to anticipate that we would see any

MiGs; we hadn't seen any in the previous few days. The flight members on this particular flight included Lieutenant Wilton "Bing" Crosby on my wing, Lieutenant Hershel "Herb" Leichty as element lead, and Lieutenant Ed Hepner on his wing. Herb was a West Point graduate and a superb pilot. He was flying aircraft number 868, the aircraft I had been flying when I shot down the MiGs on September 26th.

As we reached the vicinity of the Sui-ho Dam we paralleled the Yalu in an elongated racetrack pattern. We spotted a flight of eight MiGs coming toward us in a quartering head-on approach. We had already dropped our external fuel tanks. I made a hard turn to the right and was able to get into an advantageous position. The MIGs and our F-86s were going around in a modified Lufbery and scissors movement, up and down and back and forth, in our own version of combat maneuvering. We weren't using the commonly named techniques, just trying to outmaneuver the other fellow, and get him in our twelve o'clock position, directly in front of us. While we were going round and round with this flight of eight MiGs, Herb called out eight more MiGs trying to position themselves to fire on us. Now we were engaged with sixteen MiGs.

I was able to cut off the last man in the flight of MiGs. I was on the inside, and he could tell that I was getting in position to put a bead on him. His flight was continuing to turn to the left, and he knew that if the turn continued, he would be right in my sights, so he slid out of position off to the right as we continued our left turn. The closest thing I can compare my maneuver to is a cowboy cutting off a cow from the herd by riding in and forcing one to turn away from the herd. Once he is isolated from the herd, you can focus your attention on this one individual, and take him in for branding. I was working the same procedure on the MiG.

I was able to cut him away from the flight of MiGs while they continued to turn left. I forced him to depart from his position, and as he swung out wide he appeared to be confused as to what to do. As I lined up on him, he started heading directly into the sun. This was an old World War II trick, to head into the sun so the pilot who's trying to fire at you can't see you. But I had a radar computing gunsight, and when I put it on him I could tell it was locked on. I could see that I had him where I wanted him, and I started shooting. I give him a long burst, and my airplane slowed down; we were up around 42,000 feet and he was climbing.

The MiGs could leave us behind in a climb. Occasionally, when we'd be flying straight and level, they'd be going at the same speed but they would be climbing. If we climbed to stay with them, our speed would fall off and we would not be able to maintain position with them. Every time I took a shot at the MiG, my aircraft slowed, and I dove down to pick up airspeed, regain position, and then fire again. I could see that I was hitting his engine. Every time I hit his engine, a doughnut-shaped ring of smoke came out of his exhaust. It would come floating back and I'd fly right through that doughnut-shaped cloud. My gun camera film later showed these hits quite clearly.

I kept firing at him, and another big doughnut would come back, so I could tell I was hitting his engine. I continued to shoot and he continued straight into the sun; he made no other maneuvers. We continued in this fashion for what seemed like an unusually long period of time. But even though I'd hit him several times, we were still in the contrail level. I was flying through his jet wash, which caused my airplane to wobble around, and I had to drop my nose because I was about to stall. I increased my airspeed, closed on the MiG, pulled up behind him again, placed the gunsight on him, shot, almost stalled, and dropped my nose again. I repeated this maneuver seven or eight times, dropping down, gaining speed, pulling my nose up, and shooting. Finally, we were over the Yalu River.

We had a "hot pursuit" policy that stipulated that if we were engaged with a MiG, we could maintain contact and continue to shoot at him as long as we were in contact. But I decided it was time to turn around, as I was just about out of ammunition and approaching "bingo" fuel. I made a call over the radio, saying that I had a MiG burning over the Yalu at 42,000 feet, available to anyone who wanted to get him if he came back over the Yalu, but that we were low on fuel and had to break off. The two flights of MiGs did not follow us in pursuit. I don't know why the second flight of eight didn't follow us—if they did follow us, they were far enough back that they didn't pose a threat. The other MiGs that my MiG was flying with continued their left turn and I never saw them again.

We headed home and landed at K-13. Several other aircraft were in the air that day, and one of the flights was from the 39th Squadron. During debriefing, the intelligence officer asked what had happened, and I told him the whole story. But before we left the debriefing area, some men from the 39th Squadron came in to debrief, and one of the men—I believe the man's name was Major Vischer—said that he had seen the whole thing. He said right after I broke off and headed for home, the MiG dropped his nose, made a left-hand turn, and burst into flames. The pilot bailed out, and the aircraft headed due south towards the Cho-do Island area. The MiG was near the mouth of the Yalu when the pilot bailed out. Major Vischer told the debriefing officers his story, confirming my fourth victory.

In November the weather became much colder, and good flying days were less plentiful. We had more new pilots checking in, and we had more pilots with fewer missions, so individually we flew less often. As a result,

Cecil Foster and his F-86, the *Three Kings*, Korea, 1952.

during the entire month of November, I flew only seven combat missions. Part of that time I went on rest and recuperation (R&R) leave in Japan. All of the men in my flight went on R&R with me, and we spent three days in Japan. Japan was still an occupied country at this time, with a significant American presence throughout the city. We stayed at the American-run hotels, and spent most of our time eating good food, to make up for the less than satisfactory chow we were given in the squadron. We rode taxicabs to the zoo or the Ginza, where we went shopping. I bought pajama outfits for the boys and a set of Japanese china for my wife. While we were there, I called home and talked to Margaret, and learned that our fourth son, Ronald, had been born on the 13th of November. A few days after we returned to K-13, I received a message from the Red Cross informing me that Ronald had been born. So I had double confirmation of my son's birth. I told my wife that now that I had another son, I was going to have to shoot down at least one more MIG, because I had one for her and one for each of the other three sons. In fact, I had named my aircraft "Three Kings." Now with a fourth son I had another reason to claim another MIG.

CHAPTER 9

Ace Status

IT DIDN'T TAKE LONG after I returned from Tokyo to become an ace. It occurred during my first mission, on the 22nd of November. On this mission four flights of four F-86s had been assigned to escort an RF-80 photo-reconnaissance aircraft. I had been designated as the mission leader, and I had to figure out for myself how to set up an escort for a slower-flying photo-recce aircraft, how to disperse the flights in various positions to protect the aircraft, and how to maneuver to maintain position. I decided that when we flew with the recce aircraft, I would position my element leader and his wingman on one side of the aircraft, and I would be on the other side with my wingman. I positioned a second flight of four aircraft high on the right, a third flight high on the left, and the fourth flight farther back, in the stern position, also flying high. I briefed the mission as best I could. Actually, I was embarrassed. When I finished I felt as if I had done a highly inadequate job. But everybody seemed to be satisfied. I had no complaints from the wing commander or the group commander.

We went out, climbed in our aircraft, and took off. My flight followed the photo-recce aircraft into the air, the other flights followed us, and we all joined up. But the problem was that the recce aircraft didn't fly quite as fast as we did, and we had to maintain position by crossing back and forth, or by slowing down. The high flight was in the stern, or six o'clock position, another flight was over at the four-thirty position, and the third flight at the eight o'clock position. They kept their speed up by crossing back and forth. My element lead and I flew at a slower speed, at the same speed as the recce aircraft, and two aircraft on either side of the photo-recce aircraft also flew at a slower speed.

When we crossed the bomb line, I instructed the pilots to check their guns and assume the combat spread position. We continued north. The target that day was the Sui-ho Reservoir Dam. The recce aircraft had his assigned headings and altitudes for his photo-recce run, and our job was to protect him. When our external fuel tanks were dry, I called for all escorting aircraft to drop their external tanks. Everyone was able to jetti-son tanks except for me. I had two hung drop tanks, which was very unusual. The element leader in my flight was a newly assigned colonel, who was just getting checked out in the area. I had designated him as the alternate mission commander, and although he was new to the area, he took over the flight, and I and my wingman pulled up and away from the formation.

I flew alongside for a while as I made several attempts to shake my external tanks loose, but nothing worked. Because we believed that we would be encountering MiGs sent up to intercept the mission, we knew we should depart the area, especially since my wing tanks were still attached to my aircraft and would severely restrict my combat performance. I turned over command of the mission to the element leader and headed back towards K-13 with my wingman, Lieutenant Ed Hepner. I tried to figure out why my external tanks wouldn't shake loose. I checked every electrical connection I could think of, the circuit breakers, the switches, and I kept pushing the drop tank release button, but nothing happened. Finally, I pulled out the circuit breaker and left it out and then pushed it back in again and punched the tank release button, located on the stick, and boom! both tanks departed the aircraft. Now that I had lost my tanks I was ready for combat.

I called my element leader, telling him I had been able to drop my tanks and would try to rejoin the formation. He said that that was not a good idea because it would be too hard to catch up with them. I decided to rendezvous with them after they turned from the target and headed for home. I was heading north towards the dam at the time. As I flew north I could hear the other aircraft over the radio, giving their coded calls prior to making their turn toward the target. They completed their target run and turned to a southerly heading. Just as we began a turn to the south, Ed and I spotted a flight of four MiG-15 aircraft. We met almost head-on, and all four of them fired at us, but we weren't hit.

I initiated a climbing maneuver, using what I called a "whifferdill" maneuver, climbing, turning, and then descending to position us to the left of the flight of MIGs. They made a hard right climbing turn, which put us almost in a scissors position, but in a crossing pattern. Due to my exuberance, I guess, I performed a loose barrel roll, which allowed us to maintain airspeed but lose forward position. As a result of this maneuver

I was able to position myself to the stern, behind the last two aircraft of this flight of MiGs. I wasn't quite in their six o'clock position, but in a quartering stern position. We were engaging in normal air-to-air combat maneuvering—turning, climbing, diving, pulling hard, rolling, trying to end up in a favorable position at the right distance from the other aircraft.

I was able to get off a few shots as I was maneuvering, and we in turn were shot at as well. I didn't see any successful hits nor did we receive any hits at this time. We could tell by the movements of the MiG aircraft that they were not amateurs; they were experienced pilots and they were ready and willing to fight. As we continued to maneuver, I could hear the progress of our photo-recce mission over the radio; the flight was well on its way back to K-13. Our fuel was running low, and we needed to get out of there. I decided that now was the time to leave, and I told Ed, "Let's go!"

We both pulled into a sharp turn for K-13 at maximum speed. We looked back and saw that the MiGs were following us. We could see at least two that were approaching us, one behind each of us. They continued to gain on us until one MiG moved to within about 2000 feet of Ed, who was on my right side, and I called him, saying, "Ed, break left!" At the same time I broke right so that we could cover each other from the MiGs.

But at the same time, I learned later, he called, "I'm breaking left!" He never heard my call and I didn't hear his call, because we called at the same time, and we turned in different directions. We had been flying in a wide combat spread with me slightly in the lead on the left, and our turns brought us towards one another. Just at the moment he started his turn, Ed received some hits from the lead MiG.

He then made a transmission, "I've taken a hit!" At the same time, as I was crossing over him, the MiG that was following him saw me coming towards him, and he ceased his pursuit of Ed and flew straight ahead. As he did so, I was able to do a roll to the right, back around behind and underneath him, coming up behind him. I do not know if the MiG that was following me shot at me or not. I did not see him shoot and Ed never saw him shoot, because Ed was looking at the MiG that was on his tail. But I was able to get around behind the MiG that had shot at Ed's aircraft.

As I did, I took a shot at him, aiming by following the flight of my tracers. On my third burst I could see that I was hitting the MiG, and suddenly his airplane appeared to stop in midair. I was rapidly overrunning him. I put out my speed brakes, pulled my power to idle, came up close behind him, and fired again. I knew I was hitting his airplane. I did not see any flame, nor I did not see any action from the pilot reacting, to indicate that he knew he was being shot at. He kept going straight ahead, but he was almost stopped in midair, as if his engine had been completely knocked out. I was still overrunning him and my aircraft was rapidly approaching his exhaust pipe. When it seemed like I was going to run into him, I pushed my nose down and went underneath him.

As a result of my quick descent underneath the other aircraft I gained speed and saw that I was about to pull in front of him. I decided that was a bad idea, and I made a hard right turn followed by a hard left turn while I was below him, to kill my airspeed and to keep moving so that he couldn't get a shot at me, if he was able to do so. As I pulled off to the left, I looked up and saw him eject from his aircraft. The pilot soon dropped out of sight, and I didn't have to worry about him any more. Now I had the time to try to find out what had happened to Ed. I maneuvered around in the sky and started calling, "Where are you, Ed?" When I received no answer, I knew he'd been hit. I saw no other MiGs. The sky was empty of aircraft. I saw no explosions on the ground, I saw no fires, and I frantically looked around for some sign of my wingman.

Fortunately, within a few minutes I heard him call over the radio, "Bronco Lead, Bronco Two calling in the blind. I've been hit. My instrument panel is shot out. I don't know how much fuel I've got. My engine is running all right, but my canopy is gone, and I can't hear a thing. I'm heading for Cho-do Island and plan to eject there."

When I heard Ed's call, I thought "Thank God!" and headed towards Cho-do Island, making abrupt clearing turns, to keep myself clear of MiGs, as I headed west. I had briefed the men in my flight many times before that if they got into trouble, I would stay with them as long as I could, and that they should attempt to fly over the water, off the coast, where they could be picked up by the air-sea rescue crews. I determined that I would orbit in the area near Cho-do Island even if it meant staying there until I ran out of fuel. I tuned in Guard Channel on my radio and could hear the rescue people talking; they had already been alerted. I knew that Ed was squawking our emergency code on his IFF transponder. I heard the rescue helicopter at Cho-do Island say "We have you in sight," but he didn't answer because he couldn't hear anything. But he saw them hovering and he said, "I'm going to eject now." Then I heard the transmissions from the helicopter crew, who said they had him in sight and were in position to pick him up as soon as he hit the water. At this point I knew he was in good hands and I headed for home.

I was barely able to return to K-13 with the fuel I had remaining. And when I did taxi in and shut down my engine, I could hardly walk when I got out of the airplane. My knees were shaking and I was extremely nervous. It was the most traumatic experience I had ever had. It left me completely weak. After I landed I took the film pack out of its compartment in the nose of the aircraft. When I examined it I saw that it hadn't taken any pictures. Not one. When I looked in the aircraft maintenance log I saw that the camera had been written up at least three times previously because it wouldn't take any pictures. And each time the maintenance team had done something and signed it off as fixed. When I saw this I let out my frustration by throwing the film pack on the ground. Then I picked it up and took it into the debriefing with me. The intelligence officer said, "Your film pack has a dent in it," and I said, "Yes. I lost my temper and threw it on the ground when I discovered it didn't take any pictures."

So there was no confirmation of the aircraft I had shot down, no film to show I had shot it down, no one to say he saw the airplane go in, so I couldn't claim it. So all I could do was tell them what had happened. But we had an especially sharp Army intelligence officer assigned to our intelligence section, and he said, "I'm going up to Seoul this afternoon, and let me do some checking." As far as I was concerned that was the end of my mission; I had a good story to tell but no confirmation. I'd gotten a fifth MiG, but there was no way to prove it.

Ed Hepner was picked up and eventually came back to the flight. He was flown to Seoul first, where he was debriefed, and then he caught a flight down to K-13. I borrowed the squadron commander's jeep to go to base operations and pick him up. He stepped off the aircraft that brought him back, grinning and with a patch on his forehead. A bullet from the MiG had passed through the canopy and detonated on his instrument panel. A piece of shrapnel had passed through his helmet and struck a glancing blow to his head. When I saw him I said, "Thank God you're alive!" I was so weak that I couldn't even get out of the jeep to walk over and shake his hand. I tried to get out of the jeep, but my legs wouldn't hold me up.

I told Ed, "You're going to fly as flight leader from now on, until you get a MiG as pay back for the one that got you. Did you know that I shot that airplane down that got you?" And he said, "No, I didn't know that." Although he wasn't able to confirm my MiG, I was extremely glad to see him alive again.

Surprisingly, our intelligence officer came back four days later, on the 26th of November, and said, "I have your confirmation." He never did tell me how he got that confirmation. The intelligence channels were too secret to let us know, but there was no question that a MiG was shot down and that it was my aircraft. That was my fifth MiG. I was now officially an ace.

Needless to say, on the night that I was informed that I had become an ace, there was a party in the squadron area and good feelings were running high. I even drank a couple of beers that night. They were warm, as

Cecil Foster prior to shooting down his fifth MiG, November 1952.

usual, because there was no way to keep the beer cold, and we sat around, hollering and laughing and singing. I remember that evening very well. No pilot from the 51st Wing had reached ace status for some time, and there was no one after me for another two months. I was the 23rd jet ace in the Korean War. Dolph Overton, who was the 24th jet ace, got his fifth MiG on the morning mission of the 24th of January, and Hal Fisher, the 25th jet ace, got his fifth MiG on the afternoon of the 24th of January.

I placed Ed's name on the scheduling board as flight leader for the next few days, and when our time came to fly again, I flew the number three position. That was the position he was flying—flight leader—when we flew a mission to the Yalu River on a combat air patrol on the 6th of December. As we were cruising at an altitude of thirty-six or thirty-seven thousand feet, we spotted a lone MiG that apparently was a little out of position in a flight of four MiGS, flying along in a loose combat formation. Ed made a firing pass at this MiG and hit it; the MiG rolled over on its back, made a couple of slow rolls, then entered a spin. Ed continued firing at the MiG while I with my wingman, Lieutenant Wilton "Bing" Crosby, covered him from the rear. I kept calling to Ed that he was clear, and we followed the MiG down to about 3000 feet, when the MiG made one more slow roll and hit the ground. That MiG kill was Ed's first combat victory.

As we passed over the burning MiG, I was in a trail position, and I noticed coming from our left to our right, heading towards the Yalu River, a single MiG about 10,000 feet above us. I called out the position of the MIG, told everyone to go to full power, and because I was in the best position, I started to cut the MiG off, hoping to get a good shot. Then I saw another MiG about 1500 feet behind the first, in trail. I had a better chance of getting a shot at the second MiG, so I pulled my nose up, and started to turn inside him. As I was watching the second MiG, I saw him fire his guns at the first MiG. At first I didn't believe what I was seeing. But as I continued to watch, I saw the pilot of the second MiG shoot and hit the first MiG. I was used to the idea that American pilots shot at MiGs, but I couldn't believe MiG pilots shot at MiGs. The first MiG then rolled over and went into a descending spiral. The second MiG continued straight across the Yalu at full power.

While this unusual drama was going on, I was able to get into good position behind the first MiG and I went into a vertical spiral right behind him. As he continued in a descending spiral I was able to get several shots at him. When I flew by the first MiG pilot, before I got into firing position and right after he went into his spin, I could see him in his cockpit, wearing what appeared to be a cloth helmet of the type worn during World War II. It was not a hard hat helmet like we wore. I could see that he was moving his hands around in the cockpit; he appeared to be trying regain control of his aircraft. I also noticed that this MiG looked a little different than the other MiGs I had seen; it had several stall fins, or fences, as we called them, located at regular intervals along the wing outward from the fuselage. I had never seen these fences on any of the MiG-15s I had shot down. I was able to position myself behind him in a spiral and fire several bursts at him while he was in his spiral. I continued to pursue the MiG until I received a call from my wingman, "Bing" Crosby, who called "Pull out, Lead! You'll hit the ground!" I rolled my wings level and pulled back on the stick, as hard as I could, pulling about eight Gs, and I leveled off about a thousand feet above the ground. Even though I had been spiraling down, I had enough speed to pull out with plenty of room. I rounded up the other members of our flight, Ed Hepner and his wingman, and we flew back to K-13, full of excitement and pumping adrenaline.

After we landed, "Bing" Crosby and I discussed what we had seen, and he agreed that the MiG I had shot down (with some help from another

MiG) had distinctive stall fences on the wing. For a while we thought it was a MiG-15 that had been fitted with some experimental design to improve stability, so we said nothing at the debriefing about what we had seen. Besides, in the tumult of combat, so much is going on that it's hard to know for sure what you saw and didn't see. Some months later, the first photographs of a new MiG aircraft appeared, the MiG-17. The MiG-17 had prominent wing fences, just like those on the aircraft I shot down. When I saw the photographs, it began to occur to me that perhaps we had seen a MiG-17 on December 6th. If that was the aircraft we saw, then I could make the claim that I was the first American pilot to shoot down a MiG-17. Regardless of what kind of MiG I shot down, it was still a good day for us, for on that day, Ed Hepner shot down his first MiG and I destroyed my sixth.

CHAPTER 10

A Lull in the Action

DURING THE LATE FALL and early winter of 1952, a strike in the United States affected the production of the external drop tanks we needed for our combat missions over North Korea, and we began to run out. For a period of time we flew with only one drop tank, but were told not to drop it unless and until we engaged in active combat with MiG aircraft. Later we had to fly without any external tanks, which limited our range prohibitively. We also used some foreign-made tanks, which were shaped like cylinders, and not aerodynamically designed for high-speed aircraft. This situation presented a severe handicap for the pilots, as it significantly limited our ability to do our job. We pilots felt that we were not being supported by the people back home. We couldn't understand why there should be any reluctance to produce drop tanks, which were essential to us if we wanted to do our jobs. When our supply of drop tanks ran out, we flew without the necessary amount of fuel to conduct our combat air patrol missions. This drop tank restriction stayed with us for over a month. When we flew, we felt as if we had one hand tied behind us. It was an uncomfortable situation for us. It was all due to the fact that some people back in the States wanted more money, and knew that we needed these drop tanks badly. This predicament did not make us sympathetic to the unions responsible for this situation.

Not too long after I arrived in Korea, Margaret decided to return to Texas, and with her father's help, moved back to her parents' home in San Antonio. She was pregnant with our fourth son, Ronald, and was not having an easy time with her pregnancy. There were no military hospitals in the Midland, Michigan, area, and this was the major factor in her decision to move back to Texas. The personnel in the military hospitals in San

Antonio were a great help to her. The letters that Margaret wrote to me significantly boosted my morale during this period. She wrote me almost on a daily basis. The only time she didn't write was when she or one of the children was ill or in the hospital, and she didn't have the time to write. Of course, I didn't receive a letter every day; occasionally several days would go by when I didn't receive a letter, but on other days I would receive several at one time. I always read them in the order they were written. She kept me up to date on the events at home: how she and the children were doing, stateside news events. After I began shooting down MiGs, we began to receive newspaper coverage, and the more MiGs I shot down, the more coverage I received.

When I reached ace status, the papers in Michigan, specifically the *Detroit Evening News* and the *Detroit Free Press*, began to make an issue out of the fact that the Texas papers were attempting to claim a Michigan man as a Texas ace. And the Texas newspapers argued right back that maybe I used to be Michigan boy, but I was from Texas now, because San Antonio was listed as my home of record. I eventually settled the issue by sending a message to my wife and to the *San Antonio Evening News*, stating that I considered Texas my home state because that was where I was living and working when I was recalled to active duty.

The relationship with the press was beneficial for me in a number of ways. One of the newspaper reporters wrote to me and asked if I would write a story describing what a day in the life of a jet fighter pilot in Korea was like. I wrote several hand-written pages of description, and it was published in the San Antonio paper. The San Antonio paper also printed a story about me and my family, complete with pictures. When I reached ace status, the headlines in the San Antonio paper were the largest they had ever used. They said the only time they would use a larger print would be to announce the second coming of Jesus Christ. The press produced many articles about me and my family, mostly as a result of their own investigative work, because little information was released through military sources. Margaret and I eventually received newspaper articles and clippings from cities all across the United States and placed them in scrapbooks.

The newspaper reporters kept in regular contact with my wife, asking her if I had written to her lately, and this information was published periodically between official releases describing additional MiGs I was shooting down. This attention resulted in a tremendous amount of publicity for me personally, but didn't have much of an impact on my pay scale. Reading these stories helped to pass the time, because in reading the stories my wife sent, I could learn more about the war and my part in it than I could around the operations center of the squadron.

For the first part of my tour in Korea, my aircraft number was 738. But on one wet, rainy day a refueling truck put my airplane out of commission. He was traveling a little too fast as he approached my airplane, and as he attempted to turn to put himself in position to refuel, the truck skidded on the wet pierced steel planking, or PSP, and the rear end of the truck impacted my airplane. He hit my airplane so hard the frame was warped. My airplane had to be sent back to Japan, where it went through a major overhaul to put it back in flying condition. Several years later, I discovered that it had returned to combat status and had been assigned to another individual, and remained in combat as a serviceable flying machine.

After 738 was put out of commission, I had to wait until another pilot rotated back to the States. Eventually I received Lieutenant Kautto's aircraft, 737, after he rotated. The phrase that I had painted on 738 was "Three Kings and a Queen," in recognition of my three sons and my wife. When I lost 738, I had to find another artist to repaint 737. My wife was pregnant at the time, and I thought that if she had a girl, I would rename my airplane "Full House," because there would have been three kings and two queens. But when my fourth son was born, I changed the name to "Four Kings and a Queen." My aircraft was repainted before I left Korea, but only a few weeks before I left. Because I shot down my last three MiGs in the last three days I was there, there was no time to paint the last three stars on the side of the cockpit. Most pictures taken of the aircraft show only six stars on the aircraft instead of the nine I was finally credited with.

In December the snow fell steadily at K-13 until it was a foot and a half deep. We stood alert frequently that month, and had to preflight our aircraft while it was still dark, and then we would have to sit in the cockpit, waiting for the sun to come up. It was cold that month, miserably cold. Sitting on alert in the cold was no fun, but it had to be done. Fortunately, we were never scrambled during one of those early morning alert duties. The main reason for sitting on alert was to be prepared in case an enemy aircraft would come across at dawn to bomb or strafe, trying to catch us sitting on the ground, unprepared. I'll never forget how cold it felt at five or six o'clock in the morning. The aluminum metal of the aircraft was covered with frost. I've spent a lot of winters in Michigan and experienced a lot of cold days, but I never felt as cold as I did sitting on alert during those December mornings in Korea. In December one of my pilot school classmates, Lieutenant Joseph McConnell, was assigned to our wing; he checked out in the 25th Squadron and then was reassigned to the 39th Squadron. McConnell later became the number one ace in Korea with sixteen kills. But he extended his stay in Korea beyond the normal tour of duty, for another 25 missions, and during this time he was shot down once and was picked up out of the ocean by helicopter.

The weather was not conducive to flying, and during the month of December I flew only nine combat missions and one training mission. But December was especially noteworthy for me because I was promoted to spot captain on the 22nd of December. A spot promotion is a rank temporarily assigned when a pilot fills a position that calls for a higher rank. The individual can be temporarily promoted to the rank for that position and keep it as long as he holds that position. I had no idea that I had been recommended for the promotion, but on the 22nd I received promotion orders. The extra pay was a welcome blessing. I kept the rank until I left the theater, about one month later.

CHAPTER 11

The Final Victories

TOWARD THE MIDDLE OF January the flying weather began to improve, and our squadron pilots once again began to encounter MiGs. The squadron commander, Major Ed Heller, shot down two MiGs that month. On the 21st of January, Dolph Overton shot down a MiG, and on the 22nd Dolph and I both shot down MiGs. On the 23rd of January Ed Heller was shot down; his score at that time was three and a half MiGs, including one on the mission on which he was shot down. When he ejected he was north of the Yalu River and was taken captive by the Chinese. After the truce was signed, the pilots who were shot down north of the Yalu were not repatriated. They stayed in prison for another two years before they were permitted to return to the United States.

During the month of January, until the time I flew my final missions, there were few good flying days; I flew only ten combat missions in January. I taught ground school to pilots new to the wing, gave them theater checkouts, and led them on their first combat missions. These missions were not likely to result in actual combat engagements, so I logged them as training flights, while the others were credited with combat missions. But by January 21st I had logged 94 combat missions. During my last three days in Korea I flew four combat missions.

On a mission on the 22nd of January, I made a colossal mistake by not using my head. We spotted an enormous number of MiGs coming across the Yalu in the contrail level. My flight and some flights from another squadron were intercepting them. They were ahead of us, in a stream of aircraft, more or less, with several flights following one another in trail. The MiGs flew different formation patterns than we flew, but when they were all strung out in trail, they looked impressive. As the first MiGs came across, the flights in front of us maneuvered to engage the tail-end aircraft in the MiG stream. The lead F-86s maneuvered into position to engage the MiGs in the stern of the stream, which was the wisest and safest thing to do. But there wasn't room for all of us to swing around behind. I had a little altitude advantage, so I used this to attempt to hit the middle of the stream.

I led my flight in a descending right hand turn, and swung down to get into the middle of the stream of MiGs. I thought that by doing this I might break up their formation and then everybody would have an opportunity to shoot at a MiG, and I could hope to get one on my way through. I rolled out behind one MiG in the middle of this stream and shot a long burst into his tailpipe section from a distance of about 1500 feet. Unfortunately, this position put me about 500 or 1000 feet in front of another MiG, who immediately pulled over and started lining up on me, and when he did so, my wingman sang out, "Break left!"

I did a rolling left break, and as I did so I noticed the MiG behind me was doing a rolling turn as well, following me. My wingman said, "Keep turning, he's still on you!" That MiG stuck with me as I did a tight spiral at full speed, diving for the ground. The MiGs could outclimb us, but we could outdive them. As I pulled away from him in the dive, he pulled off and headed back towards the MiG stream and disappeared. In the meantime, I didn't know what had happened to the MiG I had shot at. But the flights that were behind me from the other squadrons, which were attacking the trailing sections of the MiG stream, saw me go in, saw me shoot, and saw the MiG roll slowly over and go into a dive. I wasn't paying attention to what happened to him, but apparently he and I were diving at the same time. But mine was a controlled dive; his wasn't. The other pilots saw him crash.

At the time, however, I didn't know what had happened. When I returned to K-13, I claimed a damaged MiG. But during debriefing, the other pilots said, "Was that you, you dumb ——? You were the one who flew right into the middle of that stream of MiGs? Well, that MiG you shot at went in." So others confirmed a kill for me that I never saw, that wasn't on my film, and that my wingman couldn't see either. That was my seventh MiG.

On the 23rd of January I flew an uneventful mission. I didn't see any MiGs. However, that was the day that Ed Heller was shot down. Dolph Overton flew two missions that day and shot down two MiGs. Dolph was the next American ace after me, reaching ace status on the next day, the 24th.

On the 24th of January I flew two missions, one in the morning and one in the afternoon. Dolph Overton, another flight commander in the squadron, who had scored his fourth kill the previous day, requested that we fly together as a flight. His request was approved. His wingman was Captain Ireland and mine was once again Lieutenant Ed Hepner. Shortly after arriving over the Yalu, we engaged some MiGs and broke off into two separate elements. These MiG pilots were good, and the result for my flight was a standoff—no hits on us and no hits on them. Later I spotted some MiGs crossing left to right ahead of and above us. I cut the rear MiG off, slid up from below, and fired a long burst from a distance of 2,000 feet. Firing my guns caused me to lose airspeed and fall out of pursuit position. While we were attempting to engage and fire, the MiGs turned north and flew back across the Yalu. I thought I had only damaged the MiG, but later, during debriefing, other pilots said that they saw this burning airplane heading in their direction, descending down through their flight of F-86s heading south. They saw him come down in a flaming descent off to the right of their formation. It went right on by them and crashed. Nobody else had shot at an airplane, and nobody else had hit one, so it had to be the one I had shot at. Dolph Overton, who had become separated from me, also scored a kill on this mission, giving him five MiGs and ace status. My score stood at eight MiGs shot down and two damaged.

On the afternoon mission I was flying as number four man in the flight; I was checking out one of our new lieutenants as an element leader. We were flying a combat air patrol when we spotted several MiGs coming across the Yalu. We engaged with the MiGs, along with some other flights of F-86s. The flight leader turned to engage the MiGs, but my new element lead swung wide and was not in position to cover the flight leader as well as he should have. We were near a flight of six MiG aircraft. We were almost line abreast with their number six man, and I kept telling the pilot flying the element lead position, "Take their element leader, the number five man. Line up with him and shoot!" But he said, "I can't. I've got this MiG over here at my seven o'clock position!" And I said, "I'm holding him off. Shoot!" But he wouldn't shoot; he kept checking the MiG at his seven o'clock position, thinking it was going to come after him.

This MiG pilot was a pretty good pilot for someone assigned to fly the "tail-end charlie" position of the flight. He tried to swing in behind my element lead, but every time he did, I swung towards him. As I did, he reversed himself and pulled back out of firing position. He knew that if he pulled in behind my element lead I would be in position to shoot at him, and he was not in position to shoot at me, because we were just about line abreast. We were just feinting at one another, like a couple of boxers sparring. Meanwhile I kept yelling for the element lead to shoot! shoot! But he

Three 51st Fighter Wing aces: Dolph Overton, lower left; Harold Fischer, top center; and Cecil Foster, right. January 1953.

wouldn't do it. Finally, in frustration, I said, "Swing to my right. I've got the lead." He swung over to my right and I said, "Watch this aircraft behind me, the tail-end Charlie," and I started to fire at the MiG in front of us. I saw my bullets hit him, but about this time the other MiG started swinging towards me, and my wingman, who was covering me, called, "Break left!" I headed back around and tried to catch the other MiG, but it turned into an on-going maneuvering exercise without much action. We didn't do much after that. As far as I knew, I had hit a MiG but I didn't know how badly I had hurt him, because we had to break off.

There were many other aircraft in the area. Some saw us maneuvering just as we saw others maneuvering too. After we landed, I claimed I had damaged one MiG as well as another I had fired at earlier. During the mission debriefing it was determined that the airplane I shot had turned, gone into a spiral, started flaming, and crashed. This was confirmed by other pilots who had witnessed the encounter. They didn't know what had happened to the MiG pilot, whether he had bailed out or not. My claim for two damaged MiGs was upgraded to one kill and one damaged. My camera film did not show that I had damaged the other aircraft, so it was not confirmed. But I did receive credit for a kill, which surprised me, because I didn't think anyone else had seen the fight. Usually there are too many other things going on for other pilots to be able to confirm another pilot's combat success. This brought my total to nine confirmed kills and two confirmed damaged MiGs, although the official USAF record shows that I was credited with three damaged MiGs. Later I held a debriefing with my young lieutenant. As far as I was concerned, he hadn't followed instructions and hadn't done his job and was not prepared to be an element leader.

At this point in time there was some jealousy among the men in the squadrons. The 16th Squadron was shooting a lot of MiGs down, but few pilots from other squadrons were having any success in attacking MiGs. Someone decided the 16th pilots were going across the river, shooting down aircraft in the traffic pattern at Antung and other airfields. As far as I was concerned, this was not true. I found out later, however, that several individuals had been going across the Yalu, some of whom were higher-ranking individuals in our squadron and wing. It was also true of the other squadrons, including those in the 4th Fighter Wing. But I was not one of the individuals involved.

So I was completely surprised when the acting group commander suddenly called in six of us pilots and said, "You men have got to have been going across the Yalu, because no one flying in the normal areas is shooting down MiGs. But you are. You are guilty of violating the border and therefore I am going to put you on orders assigning you to work with the Army, flying T-6s as forward air controllers to complete your one-year tour of duty in Korea. The only alternative to that is a court-martial."

The other five people who were in the room didn't say a word. But I looked the colonel in the eye and I said, "Colonel, I have not been going across the border. In my flight I have been flying with people who work in your headquarters, who work for you, who can tell you that I have not been going across the border. They don't owe me anything, they won't lie for me—you just ask them. They'll tell you I haven't flown across the border. So as far as I'm concerned, I'll take a court-martial."

Margaret Foster and the four Foster boys with squadron mugs, January 1953 (left to right: Cecil Jr., Bryan, Rodney, and Ronald, just born).

My response really upset the colonel, to say the least. He looked at me and said, "Are you trying to tell me you got your MiGs without going across that river?"

And I said, "Yes sir, that's exactly what I'm telling you. I have not been going across the Yalu." He said nothing for the longest time—it seemed like an hour. He stared me in the eye. But I stared right back. There was no way I was going to be accused of going across the border when I hadn't done it; I would take a court-martial first.

After about thirty seconds of staring me in the eye, he said, "All right. Get out of here. You're dismissed. All of you." We all stood up, snapped a salute, and left the room. After we left the room, the other pilots, some of them captains, all looked at me and said, "Wow. Boy. We sure didn't want to go up there and be T-6 pilots, flying as forward air controllers." They didn't say they had been going across the river, and they didn't say they hadn't been going across the river. I couldn't identify any one of them now if I tried. I was so appalled and upset because of the Colonel's threat, and because I had been suspected of doing something I hadn't done, that I wasn't paying a lot of attention to the other people who were involved. That incident made my mind up—I didn't want to fly under the command of this individual any longer. I was ready to go home.

That night an order was issued grounding the 16th Fighter Squadron for seven days. The men in the squadron were told to perform additional duties—tower officer, mobile control officer, airdrome officer, alert duties, but there was to be no combat flying for seven days. Dolph Overton had just shot down five MiGs, and he was ready to go home. I was ready to go home. So we said, why don't we go home together? I had earlier received permission from Headquarters at Seoul that I could go home when I thought it appropriate, because my wife had been very ill. She had not recovered fully after the birth of our fourth son, Ronald, who was in ill health himself. I decided that I wasn't going to wait around for a week and not fly, and I didn't want to work for the group commander any longer. I had flown 98 official combat missions, though I had flown as many as 110 missions, and I didn't feel that I was shirking my duty by leaving. "It's time to go home," I said.

CHAPTER 12

A San Antonio
"Welcome Home"

ONCE DOLPH AND I decided to leave, we moved quickly. We cleared our accounts, picked up our orders, and left the squadron. We caught a jeep to Seoul and boarded a cargo aircraft for a flight to Johnson Air Force Base, Japan, where we closed out our records. I was demoted from temporary captain to first lieutenant, placed on leave status, and sent back to the United States to await further orders. When I called my wife to tell her I was coming home, she was excited, not just because she would be seeing me again, but because there was going to be a special reception when I arrived. This sounded like fun to me, because I had never experienced any special treatment before, and I doubted I would ever receive it again.

I flew from Japan to Travis Air Force Base, near San Francisco. When I arrived, a message was waiting for me from Kelly Air Force Base. I was informed that the Vice-Commander of the Continental Division of the Military Air Transport Command, and the second-highest ranking individual on the base, had asked the officials at Travis AFB to put me on the first plane to Kelly as soon as I arrived, and if necessary, to put me on as a crew member. The reason for the special treatment was that many wounded soldiers were being flown back to the States from Korea, and then on to hospitals in the States, and passenger space on military aircraft at the time was at a premium. The C-54 aircraft I flew to San Antonio carried many wounded soldiers who were being flown to the hospitals there. There were no passenger seats available, so I was put on the aircraft as a crew member. This unusual procedure had been authorized by the general. Although I had never flown a four-engine aircraft in my life, I actually flew at the controls of the C-54 for four hours.

When I wasn't in the cockpit, I walked around the aircraft, talking to some of the wounded men who were lying in litters, stacked up in rows. Most of them were Army personnel; some were seriously injured. It was strange to talk to these men who had sacrificed their bodies in Korea and were coming home without fanfare, while I was coming home all in one piece, with no physical damage done, receiving a hero's welcome. A part of me felt guilty and a part of me felt blessed that I had been able to fly my missions successfully and return home in one piece.

An Army master sergeant sat next to me when I was sitting in one of the bucket seats along the side of the aircraft. He was in my status—not injured, just looking for a ride home. We began talking as we approached Kelly Field. We had been flying in darkness for awhile, and it was about ten o'clock at night. He leaned over to me and said, "While you were up in the cockpit, they came back and told us that there's going to be some delay. Apparently we have some hot shot pilot from Korea on board and they have to park in a special parking area so the television cameras and news reporters and local brass can get a good look at him when this hot shot pilot steps off the aircraft."

"Oh?" I said. "Well, I'll be darned." I hadn't heard the details of my reception. We landed and taxied on up to base operations. I remained seated.

The sergeant turned to me again, laughing. "I hope that hot shot pilot gets off in a hurry, because it's late and I've got some places to get to."

I said, "Me, too."

After we parked, I stayed in my seat until the flight attendant came back and said "Lieutenant Foster?" I nodded, and he said, "They're waiting for you out here with their cameras ready."

The master sergeant sitting next to me nearly collapsed in his seat. His mouth dropped open, and he was totally embarrassed. He was shocked to discover that this preparation was for me, this average-looking Air Force lieutenant sitting in the seat beside him. An officer came up the steps of the aircraft and motioned me to come out. I descended the ramp and sure enough, there were the television cameras. We were met by several military dignitaries, including Brigadier General George Cassady, the vice-commander of the Continental Division of the Military Air Transport Service. A 42-piece Air Force band played patriotic music while the newspaper and television reporters asked me questions about my tour in Korea and my flight home. And there was my family to meet me. What a glorious sight that was! My wife was wearing her prettiest dress, holding a dozen roses in

Cecil Foster returns from Korea, January 1953.

her arms. Our four sons were there with her, along with her mother, father, and grandmother. It was a glorious reunion, one of the highlights of my life, to be able to come home and see my family again, after an extended period of time away from them.

We went inside the terminal building, where the reporters asked more questions and took more pictures. When they were done, finally, I was told that we were to be escorted to my in-laws' home with a police escort. At least ten motorcycles accompanied us, and I rode in a police vehicle with the sirens going and the lights flashing. Even though it was late at night, the motorcade went through downtown San Antonio, then out to my in-laws' house on West Olmos Drive. By the time we reached their house I had been on the ground for three hours and it was two o'clock in the morning. When we went inside I found breakfast prepared, a huge meal. And of course, the newspaper reporters were there too; we couldn't do anything without having our pictures taken.

For the next ten days, I couldn't take a trip to the store without reading about it in the newspapers. And the attention continued; I was invited out to a dude ranch for a short vacation, and two breweries in town each sent two cases of beer. A local insurance company executive invited us to eat dinner at a country club, and several other businesses bought us dinners. We received piles of mail from people around San Antonio, welcoming me home and saying nice things about the work I had done. People sent clippings from newspapers in Boston, Philadelphia, Detroit, San Francisco, New York, Atlanta, and Kansas City, among others. I kept everything that people sent us and made scrapbooks for my sons.

While I was still in San Antonio on leave, the Fiesta Celebration and Parade was held and I was invited to be the Co-Grand Marshall. I rode a white horse, leading the parade, wearing a western outfit provided by one of the local stores. I was dressed to fit the part, in a beautiful shirt and pants and hat and tie and boots. The other Co-Grand Marshall was Rex Allen, a well-known country singer.

My leave was about to run out, and I hadn't received any orders assigning me to a new job, so I called Headquarters, USAF. They asked me where I wanted to go for my next assignment. I said, "Well, I'd like to keep flying F-86s." I soon received orders assigning me to fly F-86Ds at Perrin Air Force Base, near Sherman, Texas.

CHAPTER 13

Flying F-86s at Perrin

I WAS PLEASED TO BE FLYING F-86s again, and in Texas, too. But when I arrived at Perrin, I found out that the unit I was joining was flying the F-86D. The D-model was an all-weather interceptor, with afterburner, autopilot, radar scope, and electronic fuel controls. The F-86D was very different from the F-86E, the airplane I had flown in Korea. In fact when I saw one for the first time, I couldn't believe it. That was an F-86? It might look a little like an F-86 externally, but the internal configuration was totally different. The mission of the aircraft was different than anything I was familiar with as well; in the F-86D, we took off, climbed to altitude as quickly as the airplane would get us there, and then ran intercepts on whatever aircraft happened to be heading our way. The idea was that during a crisis, the aircraft we would intercept would be an enemy bomber, probably a Russian "Bear" four-engine jet aircraft. But as it turned out, the only aircraft I ever intercepted were our own American bombers. But we practiced constantly in case the Russians should come.

At Perrin I was assigned to the 3558th Flying Training Squadron. I discovered that the people assigned to the unit had primarily been multi-engine pilots who had been flying propeller-driven aircraft before they started to fly the F-86D. Most had no combat experience, no fighter pilot experience, and no jet flying time. They were afraid of the aircraft, partly because it had a bad fuel control reputation. I had not associated with pilots who thought like this before. A friend, Captain Gus Sonderman, was assigned for training in the aircraft with me. When we started our check out rides in the airplane, we found that the people who were checking us out didn't know as much about the airplane as we did. Training manuals and technical manuals were still being developed, but there was a simulator, and we practiced there using the few manuals we could find. We trained ourselves and developed our own operational and emergency procedures.

When we positioned the aircraft on the runway for takeoff, we were supposed to run the power up to one hundred percent, light the afterburner, and then hit a "lock-out" button, which electronically kept the power at one hundred percent. After we completed the takeoff and became airborne, we could then unlock the fuel controls and position the throttle normally. But many of the pilots were afraid that the electronic fuel control would fail, and they were hesitant about using the throttle lock settings. We were told that when we came in to land, we didn't want to do a go-around, because the fuel control might fail.

On my third or fourth check-out mission, I deliberately flew a bad pattern and overshot the runway so that I would have to do a go-around. I had been flying this particular aircraft for a while and knew how it was likely to perform. I called "On the go," gave it some power, and went around, flew a normal pattern, and landed. The jet engines in those days burned fuel less efficiently than they do today, so typically you would see a dark trail of exhaust smoke coming from the tailpipe. When I taxied into my parking spot, I was met by the wing commander, the wing safety officer, the group commander, and a maintenance officer, all wanting to know what was wrong with the airplane.

I said, "Nothing."

"Well, why did you make a go-around?" they asked.

"Well, my pattern wasn't right, so I made a go-around."

They looked at me, then they talked among themselves for a bit, shaking their heads, and then they got in their vehicles and drove off. Apparently no one had ever made a go-around before, and they assumed I had had some kind of emergency.

The remainder of my checkout and training in the airplane was uneventful; there were no problems. Gus Sonderman and I went up together and flew intercepts on each other with the assistance of the ground controller on the ground control intercept, or GCI, site. After our practice intercept mission was over we flew aerobatics to maintain our combat proficiency as much as we could. The aircraft was a good airplane. It was heavier than the F-86E and F, and though it didn't maneuver as promptly due to its greater weight, it could fly faster, especially with the afterburner lit. With the speed brakes extended in afterburner, it would turn in a tighter radius than the E or F models.

I was told that many of the pilots in our sister squadron, the 3556th FTS, were hesitant to enter a loop in the F-86D unless they had the afterburner going. Then they would put the airplane in a dive, go as fast as they could go, then pull back, and just barely make it across the top of the loop, almost in a stall. They refused to try a loop without using afterburner. I had been flying the airplane long enough by then that I knew I could fly a loop with normal power. And then I tried to do it in idle power. I went up to a safe altitude, leveled off at normal power, pulled the throttle back to idle, let the nose drop, and picked up 400 knots. Then I pulled back with a 4G pull, held 4Gs until coming across the top, eased off to about 1G, let the nose fall through, and completed my loop. I came across the top at the same speed I would have had with the afterburner going.

I decided I would try two consecutive loops in idle power. I leveled off in normal power, retarded the throttle to idle, dropped the nose, picked up 400 knots, pulled 4Gs, and came across the top, released the back pressure, and let the nose fall through, but this time I headed down again. I picked up 400 knots again, and did another loop, no problem at all. I told the other instructors there was no reason to fear the airplane. It would perform well if they planned their maneuvers. I said I had looped the airplane in idle power.

They said, "No way." They said it was "absolutely impossible" to loop the airplane in idle. I said I would be glad to show them how. One day I was invited down to the 3556th, and I gave a briefing on how to do a loop in idle. But they refused to believe it was possible. I said, "Well, go up with me and fly my wing. I'll show you how to do it." I finally convinced three pilots to accompany me.

But when we got to altitude, they refused to follow me. "Go into trail position," I said. No way, they said, they didn't want to stall out. "All right," I said finally. "You fly in the area and watch me while I do it."

While they were watching, I flew two loops in idle. When we got back on the ground, they refused to believe what they had seen. But they had seen it done. I had told them how to do it. I had demonstrated it for them. I explained to them that the maneuver was a function of G-force. You weren't going to cover the same amount of sky as you would with the afterburner lit; with afterburner on you were going to make a *greeaat* big monstrous loop. Without afterburner, in idle, you would make a much smaller loop. They said, "Yeah, but...." Needless to say, after that double loop in idle power, my name was spread around the base as somebody who was a bit of a fool but who could do a maneuver nobody else was willing to try. I'm not sure how many people believed the maneuver was feasible. My squadron was willing to believe it, however.

The instructors at Perrin were trying to develop our proficiency in firing rockets, because we were scheduled to compete in an Air Defense meet at Tyndall Air Force Base, Florida. Prior to going to Tyndall, however, we flew to an airfield at Yuma, Arizona, to practice firing live rockets at towed targets. We were one of the first units to attempt to do this. The first time I fired a live rocket at a towed target, I got a successful "Phase 2" firing, which was the first hit on a towed target by a line pilot (as opposed to a test and evaluation pilot). A "Phase 2" firing indicated firing on the target aircraft with the reticle sight primarily.

We then flew out of Foster Air Force Base, near Victoria, Texas. At Foster Field we practiced firing rockets at targets towed by B-29s over the Gulf of Mexico, developing the proper techniques for maximum scores. We flew intercepts using 24 folding fin aerial rockets (FFARs) against the towed targets, nylon sleeves measuring 6 feet by 20 feet with metal reflectors. We were guided on our B-29 intercepts by radar ground-controlled intercept (GCI) sites located along the Gulf of Mexico. On one of my passes, I registered the first "Phase 3" firing direct hit on a towed target by a Perrin pilot. In a "Phase 3" firing, the reticle in the sight was replaced with a more accurate line and dot type sighting system; the "Phase 3" firing system occurred after the attack aircraft proceeded through the "Phase 2" sequence. The B-29 that was towing the target brought it back and dropped it at an abandoned airfield near the coast, where recovery crews were waiting to pick up the target and bring it in for examination. Our recovery crew looked all over that airfield for the "rag" (our word for the target sleeve) and couldn't find it. When they came back and said they couldn't find the target, we decided to look for it again, since we thought it might be important historically.

I told them to go back out to the recovery field and I would fly one of the F-86s over, locate the target from the air, and show them where it was. When I flew to the field I could see where it was and flew a crossing pattern right over it. I flew over it in one direction, turned 270 degrees and flew back across in another direction, forming a cross right over the target; where my paths crossed was where the target was located. I could see the men sitting on a fence watching me fly. I assumed they didn't understand what I was doing, so I repeated the pattern. I kept flying lower and slower until suddenly I realized I was too low and too slow. I was approaching a fence at the end of the field where the target was located, and I wasn't sure I could clear it.

I slammed the throttle into afterburner and fortunately was able to maintain airspeed and altitude above the ground. I estimated I was within about four feet of the ground before the aircraft picked up speed and started to climb again. I climbed on out, climbing and circling until I had lots of altitude, and as I did, I noticed that the men had picked up the target. They had stopped what they were doing while I was making passes, because they thought I was putting on a show for their benefit. I darned near killed myself thinking they didn't know where the target was. I *would* have killed myself if I'd been just a little lower and slower. Although the F-86D provided good acceleration, I was way behind the power curve when I applied power. As a result of that incident, we developed procedures for dropping, identifying, and locating targets, so we didn't have that problem again.

On another mission, I took off loaded with 24 folding fin aerial rockets on the aircraft. We flew out over the bay under GCI control into the target towing area, where the B-29 was "dragging the rag." I had just entered the target area at 20,000 feet when I heard a loud "Bang!" and I immediately knew I had a problem. The aircraft started shuddering and the engine temperature started rising rapidly. I retarded the throttle to see if the engine would run more smoothly. I turned towards Foster Field, pulling the throttle back until it was in the idle position, but the engine was still vibrating badly. The vibration was worse than driving a car with a flat tire. The aircraft was vibrating so badly that I was afraid the hydraulic lines would break, and I needed hydraulics to operate the flight controls, gear, and flaps. I was worried also that the fuel system would spring a leak and cause a fire, so I decided to shut down the engine.

I aimed for Foster Field intending to deadstick the aircraft in for a landing. I could see the field in the distance, but I soon realized I was not going to make it without power. I made a 180 degree turn, and told the pilot in a chase aircraft, a T-33 flown by another Perrin pilot, that I would try to make it into an abandoned field on the coast where the B-29s had been dropping their targets. This field was closer, and I was pretty sure I could make it in there. The field was closed; there was no tower, no aircraft, no activity of any kind, but the runway was long enough and in reasonably good shape. I set myself up for a straight-in approach, and it appeared I would have enough altitude to make it. As I approached the end of the runway, I noticed a marshy area, a bog with a small lake in it ahead of me. I didn't care for the idea of crashing with a load of armed rockets on board, so I decided to jettison the rocket pod. I hit the switch and it left the aircraft without a problem and fell into the lake.

I came in "over the fence," on short final, turning slightly to line up with the runway. The aircraft touched down and I put the brakes on and brought it to a stop. I opened my canopy, looked back and saw flames coming out of the side of the aircraft. I disconnected from my parachute, unhooked the leg and chest straps, jumped over the side of the aircraft without benefit of a ladder, and landed on the asphalt. I didn't break any bones, but my ankles were sore for weeks. I ran some distance from the aircraft, not knowing what would happen next. But as I stood there watching, the fire went out. The fire I had seen was fuel that had puddled in the aft section of the engine; it eventually burned itself out. Afterwards, I discovered that I had lost some turbine wheel blades, or "buckets," which had been thrown out of the engine and through the side of the fuselage when the engine exploded. The buckets on the turbine wheel compress the air as it passes through the engine and produce engine thrust. I had lost a big chunk of the turbine wheel and the buckets associated with it.

I was soon joined by the chase pilot, who also landed at the abandoned field, who was glad to see that nothing serious had happened. Soon some security police arrived along with some maintenance men. I climbed in the back seat of the T-bird and got a ride back to Foster Field. The aircraft had to be repaired on the strip of the abandoned airfield, so that operation required a little extra work on the part of the maintenance men.

Occasionally, when we flew practice intercept missions, we would have a little extra time and fuel, and to entertain ourselves, we flew low over Matagordo Island, a long off-shore island located off the mid-central coast of Texas. No one lived on the island, but the island was used for grazing cattle. There were no trees on the island, as I recall, just tall grass and a few bushes, rocks and boulders. With no obstructions, we could buzz the beaches and not worry about dodging natural obstacles.

One day after I had fired my rockets I decided to make a pass down Matagordo Island. I dropped on down to a good low pass altitude, somewhere around five or six feet off the deck. I was whipping across the central part of the island at about 400 knots when suddenly, in the middle of a patch of tall grass right in front of me, a large longhorn bull raised his head. He must have heard the sound of my aircraft just as I came up on him, and he reared himself up to his full height. All I could see was this large head with two large eyes and these huge, long horns. I frantically pulled back on the stick, thinking, "Oh no, I'm going to have longhorns sticking out of my engine compartment when I land. If I land." Apparently, at the last fraction of a millisecond, he must have dropped his head down again, because as I blasted over him the thunk I expected to hear never occurred. I pulled the aircraft up to a safe altitude, pulled the throttles back, and headed back to the field to land. That was the last time I buzzed Matagordo Island.

CHAPTER 14

Intercept Pilot,
Air Defense Command

Although flying in the States was less hazardous than flying in Korea, it could still be dangerous, as I found out after I was assigned to fly F-86Ds. I was stationed at Perrin for three years, from March of 1953 to April of 1956, and while I was there, many of the pilots who had been in the 16th Fighter Squadron in Korea came through our program, upgrading or transitioning into the F-86D. One of those was a special friend of mine, Captain John Tee, who was promoted to Captain at the same time I was, April 1st, 1953. He completed his check-out and was assigned to our squadron. One day he was flying on an initial approach at 1500 feet, from the north, over Lake Texoma, a large lake on the Texas-Oklahoma border. When he was over the middle of Lake Texoma, his engine quit. He stayed with the aircraft until he was over the south shore of the lake, and then he ejected.

He ejected safely and his parachute opened, but a strong wind from the south carried him back into the lake. After he hit the water, the wind kept his parachute inflated and dragged him almost the full length of the lake. When we found his body, he was still in his parachute; he had been unable to release the parachute harness. John was an excellent swimmer, and I am certain that if he had known more about escaping from his parachute in the water, he would have survived. That was one time when I wished we had had more training in water survival techniques. But when you're flying over Texas and Oklahoma, you don't think about needing water survival skills.

It became painfully evident to me during the early part of my training at Perrin that we needed covers for our radar scopes in the aircraft.

Later we were provided with something we called the "muff," a radar scope cover which prevented the sunlight from washing out the returns on our radar scopes. But when we first flew with these radar scopes, sunlight often reflected directly from the glass surface of the radar scope in the cockpit. One day, as I was flying a radar intercept mission, I turned the aircraft away from the sun, and the light from the sun reflected off the surface of the scope and blinded me. I was looking at the radar returns on the set at the time. The sun hit the surface of the scope, which was shaped in such a way that it intensified the beam of sunlight, and went into my left eye. I felt the beam in both eyes, but the most intense amount of light went into my left eye.

Momentarily I was blinded in both eyes. Everywhere I looked, all I could see was white. I reached over and put the airplane on autopilot—we had autopilots in the D models. For a few moments I panicked, wondering, "How can I fly this airplane when I can't see?" Gradually the sight returned to my right eye. But I could see nothing out of my left eye and I knew I'd better get the airplane on the ground. I terminated my intercept mission, flew the aircraft back to Perrin, and landed using my right eye only. I told the squadron commander what had happened and went to the flight surgeon.

The flight surgeon checked my eyes and said that the damage to my eyes was similar to the damage I would have received if I had looked directly into sunlight. But there wasn't much he could do; we just had to wait and let nature take its course. I was temporarily grounded, and I returned to the flight surgeon for a weekly check-up. My right eye soon returned to normal, and I gradually gained my peripheral vision in my left eye. Every time I returned to the flight surgeon he would ask how I was doing and give me different sight tests. Finally, I asked, "What's the prognosis on my eyes?" The flight surgeon shrugged and said, "If it doesn't clear up in six weeks, you will be permanently grounded."

I didn't like the sound of that. So I learned to rely on the peripheral vision in my left eye. If I looked directly at an object with my left eye, I would see a frying-pan-shaped blind spot. The handle of this pan-shaped spot went right through the center of my field of vision. The remainder of the blind spot was off slightly to the right of center of my vision. If I looked at a letter on an eye chart, I would look at the bottom part of the letter and I could see the entire letter. Not looking directly at it but just below it, I could see it. I learned how to work around my visual handicap, and eventually read the chart and returned to flying status. Up to this time I had had excellent eyesight. While I was in Korea, for instance, my eyesight was about 20/15. From then on, I placed increased strain on my right eye to compensate for the loss of vision in my left eye, and I soon had to resort to wearing glasses. But that blind spot remained. If the flight surgeon had known how badly my vision had been affected, I might not have been able to continue on flying status, and my flying career would have terminated at that time. But it wasn't. I continued flying and had a successful flying career during the rest of the time I was in the Air Force.

My fifth son, David, was born while we were stationed at Perrin, on the 16th of September, 1954. When Margaret went into labor, we piled the children into the car and drove out to the base hospital. I was able to park the car almost exactly under the window of the labor room in the hospital. I moved between Margaret, to comfort her during the early stages of her delivery, and the window, to keep an eye on our children, who were waiting more or less patiently in the car. It was a difficult delivery. David was unusually large when he was born, and Margaret is only four feet eleven inches tall. When she was in labor she experienced severe pain, and she occasionally grabbed me or my uniform. At one point she tore off one of my uniform epaulets.

In April of 1956 I received orders transferring me from Perrin to the 324th Fighter-Interceptor Squadron at Westover Air Force Base, near Springfield, Massachusetts. I flew to Westover in an F-86D about a month before my transfer date to look over the base and meet the people I would be working with. I discovered that with the exception of the squadron commander, the operations officer, and two of the flight commanders, all of the rest had come through the Perrin checkout program, and several of them had been my students. When I arrived at Westover I was assigned as the training officer, and continued the training program we had been running at Perrin. Many of the men in the squadron were academy graduates, some from West Point, some from Annapolis. They had chosen to enter the Air Force rather than the Army or Navy. This was in the years before the Air Force Academy had been completed, and each year a certain number of West Point and Annapolis graduates could enter the Air Force.

After I had been in the squadron about a year, in 1957, we were hit with an ORI—an operational readiness inspection. This test included written examinations and flying examinations. The flight examination was flown as closely as possible to combat conditions. As a part of the ORI, some of the large bomber aircraft from Strategic Air Command (SAC) flew down into the northeast portion of the United States from northern Canada. The air defense system was supposed to detect these invading aircraft, identify them, and launch intercept aircraft. This exercise was conducted during the nighttime hours. During the night I flew we were experiencing bad weather as well—clouds, thunderstorms, rain. I was sitting on alert with a flight of two wingmen when we received the call to scramble.

We took off, followed the ground controller's instructions, and began our intercept run on a SAC bomber. It was dark and hard to see, so I can't say for certain what kind of bomber it was, but I believe it was a B-47. After we were cleared to intercept the aircraft I placed the other aircraft in my flight in a staggered trail sequence behind me. After being vectored to the immediate vicinity of the bomber, I noticed a blip on my radar that showed the target was about sixty degrees off to our left, low. We were approaching the target at a rapid rate. I gave a call to my flight, made a quick left diving turn, held the target momentarily at the twelve o'clock position, and then made a hard right turn to line up for a ninety degree intercept off the target's beam. Frontal intercepts were usually successful, but they could be tremendously scary and hazardous, especially for the crew of the target aircraft. However, in spite of the night and bad weather, I had a contact, was locked on to it, and was ready to run an intercept.

But my flight members couldn't see the target. They had me on their radar but they couldn't locate the target. I went into the Phase 2 firing mode, then Phase 3, completed a simulated firing, and broke left. When I broke, all I could see was a vague shape, a blur. I knew from practicing during daytime conditions that our position when we simulated firing our rockets was so close to the target aircraft that it was a frightening experience, and I didn't want to think how close I was flying to this target aircraft at night, even though I couldn't see it in the darkness. I was credited with a "kill," but the other two aircraft in my flight registered misses.

The next day we flew to a live firing range off the Massachusetts coast, near Otis Air Force Base, to run intercepts on and execute firing passes at towed targets. We were hoping to earn an ADC "A" award; to do so, we had to fly a specified number of intercepts and achieve a 95% successful intercept rate. While we were talking on the ramp at Otis, we realized that we needed two more attempts and successes to achieve this mark. We barely had the time to make the effort, but we decided we'd try for it.

The squadron commander, Major Marvin Glasgow, and I flew this mission together. His aircraft was fully refueled, but when the ground personnel began to refuel my airplane, they were able to load only a small amount of fuel before the fuel truck ran dry. We waited until the last possible second, but they couldn't find any more fuel for us. According to my fuel gauges, I had 1700 pounds of fuel on board. That wasn't much fuel; normally we entered the traffic pattern to land with 1200 pounds. But I said I would attempt an intercept. I thought that if I planned the flight carefully, I could make it.

We fired up our aircraft, taxied out, received our take-off instructions, and away we went. I was on the squadron commander's wing. He used afterburner on takeoff, but I used normal military power—100%. I didn't fall too far behind him, because I was light enough that I could almost keep up with him. As soon as we were airborne, I told him to fly the mission, and that I would position myself at an appropriate distance from his aircraft. He handled all the radio communications and responded to the directions from the GCI controller. When we started talking to the GCI controller, I said, "I'm going to have to make one pass, and it has to be from left to right because the right side of my scope is completely blank." That was because we had a slight mechanical problem that the maintenance men hadn't had time to fix. "And," I added, "immediately after the termination of intercept, instead of making the normal break to the left, I'm going to break right to return to base because I'm low on fuel." I wasn't through yet. "And I'd like to catch the target as close to the west side of the range as possible." That would give me an altitude advantage to use when I returned to land at Otis; I thought I might have to fly a flameout pattern at Otis.

There was a long pause, as if the ground controller was absorbing this information, and then he said, "Roger."

The ground controller did his job perfectly, guiding toward the target aircraft without a problem. The squadron commander got his hit on the "rag," the target towed by the range aircraft, and I got my lock on and called Phase 3 Firing. "Splash the target," I called. As soon as I called "Splash," I pulled the throttle all the way back to the idle position, turned hard right, and started gliding to the airfield at Otis. At this point I was at 33,000 feet, down to about 500 pounds of fuel, and quite a way from the runway—approximately 70 miles. But the D-model had an excellent glide ratio. I glided on into the coast and established a high SFO—simulated flameout—pattern over the field. I called the tower and said, "Don't let anyone on the runway. I'm low on fuel and I'm making an SFO, but I'm going to land out of it." Usually SFOs were practice maneuvers with the aircraft adding power and going around just prior to landing, but this time I had no choice: I had to land.

I landed with about 150 pounds of fuel remaining. I was able to taxi the aircraft into the parking area before the engine flamed out. We reached our required amount of successful intercepts, and we got our ADC "A" award, one of the first ever awarded. During this ORI, I was scheduled to fly seven flights, flew seven intercepts, and was credited with seven "kills." To the best of my knowledge, that record—of seven successful intercepts for seven attempts, including four live firings, during an ORI—was never

Cecil G. Foster. Photograph by Maurice Constant, 1957.

surpassed, never equaled, and never approached by any fighter interceptor crew member. That record stood until the time that EDAF, the Eastern Air Defense Force, went out of existence.

While I was assigned to the 324th Fighter Interceptor Squadron, Air Defense Command developed three skill ratings: Qualified, Skilled, and Expert. I was able to count the time I was alert-ready at Perrin AFB in the training squadron towards the two years of combat-ready status that was required to be eligible for the ADC Expert rating, and I earned the first Expert rating given in the ADC Eastern Area Defense Force.

While I was at Westover a number of West Point graduates were assigned to my flight. One was Lieutenant Robert E. Chapman, who later became a brigadier general.

One day another Academy graduate assigned to me was flying on a mission in a flight that I was leading and we were doing some aerobatics and some one-on-one combat tactics training at Westover. He somehow lost control of his airplane, it fell out of control and struck the ground, and he was killed. He was the only wingman in any of my flights that I lost in peacetime flying.

At one point I needed to practice my instrument flying skills and scheduled myself to fly in the back seat of a T-33 while we flew as an intercept target for F-86s. We were climbing out from Westover on a north-north-east heading. We climbed to about 35,000 feet, while I practiced my instrument training under the hood. Suddenly I heard a loud "Bang!" I recognized the noise from my previous F-86 experience: our engine was gone. I immediately folded the hood back so I could see out of the cockpit and told the pilot in the front seat that I would take over control of the airplane. As an instructor pilot, I was in charge of the flight.

I remembered from the morning briefing that the jet stream was sitting right over the top of the state of Massachusetts; the wind was blowing us to the east at 175 knots. The recommended glide speed in a T-33 is much less than 175 knots. I reduced the throttle setting to less than 50%, and the engine vibration smoothed out a little. We had tip tanks with lots of fuel in them. I turned back towards Westover, but I could see that we weren't making progress. We were floating above the same spot on the ground and weren't moving forward at all. I increased my glide speed to about 165 knots, but that didn't help. If anything, we were going backwards. I could tell we were never going to make it to Westover, and I decided to aim for Bedford-Hanscom Field, on the west side of the Boston area.

With the tail wind behind me, and gliding at 165 knots, I was suddenly making an excellent ground speed—well over 300 knots, and I was over Bedford in no time at all. We contacted the tower operators and told them the nature of the problem. I retarded the throttle to idle to reduce the vibration, but the engine exhaust gas temperature—the EGT—had increased to the danger area, so I shut the engine down. Now we were flying an Air Force glider, and it was uncomfortably quiet in the airplane with the power off. We were over Bedford at about 20,000 feet, and I made a series of descending turns prior to landing. The tower operators suggested we drop our tip tanks in an orchard about seven miles from the field. I dropped my tanks at 7500 feet and reached high point for my flame out pattern in good shape.

I made my final 360 degree circle over the field, and as we came over the end of the runway I told the Lieutenant in the front seat to bring the aircraft in for a landing. We rolled to a stop and opened the canopy just as our battery went dead. The ground personnel towed us in to the parking ramp. Once again a turbine wheel in the engine had failed. The Air Police were kind enough to drive us back to Westover.

While I was at Westover I received a letter from Headquarters USAF requesting me to report to the Pentagon, in Washington DC, to have an official photograph taken for the Air Force archives. I was one of several individuals who were asked to report to Washington for this purpose. The man who took these pictures for the Air Force was Maurice Constant, a world-famous photographer who had taken pictures of presidents, prime ministers, and kings and queens. I have to say that the photograph was nicely done, one of the best I've ever had taken. After I returned to Westover I was notified that I had been selected for a Regular commission in the Air Force but needed to pass a physical examination before I could accept it. This physical examination was much more thorough than the normal flying physical. I had to take an electrocardiogram, or EKG, which I had never done before. As a result of this exam, I discovered that I had what was called a first degree heart block. It was a minimal condition, but it was necessary for me to obtain a waiver, not only to receive my regular commission, but more importantly, so that I could continue flying. Happily for me, a waiver was granted, and I was appointed a regular officer in the United States Air Force and was able to continue on flying status.

CHAPTER 15

Life in North Africa

D URING THIS TIME the American Air Force presence in Europe was being increased noticeably, and our squadron was alerted for rotation overseas. The entire unit was to be moved, including dependents, to Sidi Slimane, Morocco. Fortunately we were given several months' notice to prepare for the move. Prior to leaving we prepared our aircraft for transfer to a squadron in Knoxville, Tennessee. Once our aircraft were disposed of, we packed our household goods and office records for transfer overseas. We were transferred en masse in a group of six C-121s, the old Lockheed Constellations. Our families traveled with us on these airplanes.

We departed about ten o'clock one morning; each of the C-121s took off, one after the other, and headed for Morocco. When we landed at Sidi Slimane, the customs personnel told us to unload our bags and suitcases from the airplane and lay them out for inspection on the tarmac. Even though the customs people worked quickly, there were six airplanes full of military and civilian personnel, and it took some time for the customs people to process our luggage and hold baggage. Then we were loaded on busses and driven into the town of Port Lyautey, or Kenitra as it's called today. There we were billeted in hotels. That sounds like it was a pleasant situation, but it wasn't so pleasant for a family of seven, which was the size of my family. With such a large family, I needed three hotel rooms. Feeding seven people on the local economy was an expensive proposition, and although the government did repay me a good portion of the money I spent, it didn't repay me for all of it.

Initially, the men in the unit commuted from the hotel to the air base on buses daily. My car, which I had shipped over six weeks before we left, arrived soon after we did, and I traveled to the port facility and drove it back to Port Lyautey. Now my family enjoyed greater mobility. One of the benefits of living in Morocco was the opportunity to visit many scenic and interesting places, like Tangiers, Casablanca, and Marrakech. We also traveled to Spain and Portugal, where we visited Granada, Seville, and Algeciras. This was an exciting time for our children, who had never been overseas before.

The children rode buses to attend school on base. At first a Moroccan armed guard rode on the school buses, but he was later replaced by an American military policeman. We finally were assigned quarters on the air base at Sidi Slimane, and were able to move out of the hotel where we had been living since our arrival. In our house on base were some windows in a transom at the end of the hallway that were about eight inches high and extended the length of the living room. On the other side of this transom was the garage. One night one of my sons, Rodney, the middle son, got up to go to the bathroom. As he went into the hall, he looked up and saw, on the other side of the transom windows, a man with a knife in his mouth looking into the interior of the house.

My son, scared to death, couldn't move. He was petrified with fear. He finally forced himself to turn and let out a yell: "Help!" We jumped up out of bed wondering what was the matter. By the time we ran out in the hall, the man had gone—jumped off the roof and disappeared into the night. Even though it scared poor Rodney to death, we were thankful that he had gotten up, because the intruder was forced to leave the premises. Who knows what his intentions had been? At that time it was easy to enter the base. Only a few strands of barbed wire were strung around the perimeter of the base. If an intruder wanted to steal something large, all he had to do to enter the base property was cut a few wires. While we were there, bicycles were stolen, even military vehicles were stolen; they were driven through the wires, onto the local highway, and off into the night.

Shortly after we arrived, we were notified that new F-86s were being prepared for us to fly, but we had to pick them up in Italy, where they were located. Gradually, in groups of two and three, we would catch a ride on a cargo aircraft to Italy, check out some aircraft, sign for them, and fly them back to Sidi Slimane. Our route of flight took us along the coast of Italy, over to Spain, and then down the coast to Morocco. We rendezvoused at Moron Air Base in Spain, and then flew into Sidi Slimaine as a complete squadron. It wasn't long before we were operationally ready as a fighter squadron and were on alert duty.

During one of the missions we flew out of Sidi Slimane, one of our lieutenants experienced a problem with his airplane; his engine failed in flight. I don't remember whether he lost a turbine wheel or not, but he had to shut it down. I flew on his wing trying to assist him as he glided back to Sidi Slimane, following the most direct route. When we passed through the 5000 foot mark, I told him that he needed to make his decision now: he needed to decide to stay with the airplane or eject so that he would have time for his parachute to deploy safely. The lieutenant seemed unsure as to what he should do, and finally asked me what I would do. As pilot of the aircraft he had the ultimate authority to decide whether to leave or stay with the airplane. I looked at the field off in the distance and I looked at our rate of descent, and it seemed to me that we were going to be about a quarter mile to a half a mile short of making it to the runway. I said, "I don't think you will quite be able to make it to the runway, so I recommend you eject."

He didn't say yes, no, or anything. The second I said I thought he should eject, Pow! Out he went. The canopy flew off, his ejection seat left the aircraft, and his parachute deployed. The airplane landed in a dump about a mile or so from the end of the runway. The airplane turned before it crashed. I recall that incident because it was the only time anyone ever asked me whether he should stay or leave a disabled airplane. But he followed my advice in a hurry.

I had been at Sidi Slimane about a year when the squadron commander, Major Marvin Glasgow, was assigned to the 316th Air Division at Rabat. He decided to take some people from Sidi Slimane with him up to Division headquarters, and I was one of the two individuals he asked to accompany him. I went up as chief of the fighter operations branch in the operations division of the Air Division headquarters, along with Lieutenant Robert Chapman, who was a member of my flight and who later retired as a brigadier general. The three of us formed a nucleus of knowledgeable people who knew the aircraft and the mission very well. We supervised the crews of the 316th Air Division for the next year.

We received orders to disband the 316th Air Division by June of 1960, and once again I had the experience of deactivating a unit, which we did successfully. When we left Sidi Slimane, we turned the air base over to the Moroccan government with everything on it in working order. Every piece of equipment on that base was in working shape, from the radios in the towers to the telephone system. There wasn't one light bulb burned out, and every faucet worked; there wasn't a drip. Later I heard that we hadn't been gone from the base two days before MiGs landed on the base and the Russians, who were providing equipment to the Moroccan government, were enjoying our ship-shape facilities.

While I was working at Division headquarters, an incident occurred at Rabat, involving my family, as we were preparing to leave. My wife and

I and our children were living in a villa in town. Our villa was a nice place, located close to Embassy Row. It was a large house and we enjoyed living there. A Moroccan worked for us on a full-time basis. One morning, about six weeks before we were supposed to depart, we all woke up with terrific headaches. When I went into the kitchen, I suddenly noticed that something was wrong. The louvers that were on our kitchen door had been cut and slashed with a large knife. Some of them had been cut completely through. I looked around the house but didn't notice anything out of the ordinary at first.

About this time the children were getting ready to board the school bus, and they needed lunch money for school. The finance office at Rabat had already closed; we had received our pay in cash so we would have it before we left. When Margaret went into the bedroom to get her purse, it was gone. We started to look for it. In the bedroom where two of my sons were sleeping was a linen closet; it was open and in a mess. When we checked the kitchen again we noticed that someone had tried to come in under the sink, which led to an exterior entrance. I checked around some more and noticed that a door to the top of the villa, which was supposed to be locked, was open slightly. I stuck my head out and looked around; on the roof of the next villa over was my wife's purse, with the contents scattered over the roof. But her money was gone.

I called the military police and the civilian police. They dusted the area completely, checking for fingerprints. They determined that one of the men who had robbed us had tried to cut his way in through the louvers, and another man had climbed up a small fire escape metal ladder on the outside and had entered the house through the top door opening. Once in the house, they grabbed a pillowcase from a linen closet in one of the children's bedrooms and used it to haul the money out.

The police told us that we had been lucky, for if any one of us had moved, the robbers might have placed pillowcases over our faces and slit our throats. These robbers were professionals, because they apparently had dispensed some kind of gas in our rooms which caused us to oversleep and which had caused the headaches when we woke in the morning. They apparently saw my wife's purse and decided that was what they wanted, grabbed it and left. They didn't look around any further. If they would have, they would have discovered that her purse held only half of our cash; the other half was in my wallet on a dresser in our bedroom.

The Moroccan police eventually interrogated our houseboy. When the Moroccan police interrogated someone, it wasn't a pretty sight; they were rough. Before they went to talk to him, they told us that if he was still in the country they would find him within hours. Sure enough, within an hour and a half, they found him. I learned later that they searched his place but didn't find anything. The only items they found were the things we had given him to take home with him, including clothing and some personal items. But they didn't find any money. I don't believe he took the money, and they never discovered what happened to our money. They gave him some hard treatment, but he never admitted a thing, and I never believed he had anything to do with the robbery.

Shortly thereafter we learned that he had retained a lawyer and was going to sue us for falsely accusing him of stealing our money. But I was careful when I talked to the police and never said that I thought he had taken the money. When they asked questions about our houseboy I answered them, but I never said I thought he had done it.

The day after we were robbed I decided to hire a Berber guard to serve as a night watchman. He stood watch over our house every night until the time that we left Rabat. We felt much more secure knowing he was standing guard at night. But I'm not sure how secure we really were, because one time I caught the guard dozing off. But he was there every night, he was visible to anyone who walked by, and we weren't bothered with any more robbers.

As soon as our furniture and household goods were packed and picked up, we moved into a hotel in Rabat. We stayed in the hotel until the day we rotated back to the States. When departure day arrived, we boarded a bus for Nouasseur Air Base, where we were to be airlifted back to Charleston Air Force Base, South Carolina. We loaded all five children on the bus, threw on all our suitcases, and rode the bus to Nouasseur. When we arrived at the terminal, I unloaded the luggage and carried it into the terminal. We had two hours to wait, and we decided to get something to eat. About this time our oldest son, Cecil, said that he didn't feel well. My wife and I looked at each other. She said, "Oh no, don't say that. You're fine." After we had eaten a little bit of breakfast, he said once again, "I don't feel good." My wife felt his forehead and announced, "He's got a fever."

We took our son to the base hospital, where the doctor checked him and said, "He can't fly. He's got pneumonia." Flying to the United States was out of the question. But we had been waiting for some days for seven seats on a passenger aircraft to carry us back to the States, because space was hard to find.

I immediately caught a ride back to the passenger terminal where I reclaimed our luggage to keep it from being loaded on the aircraft and canceled our reservation. Then I went to base housing and obtained temporary housing until Cecil recovered from pneumonia, which took about a week. But once the doctor said he was well enough to fly we had to wait another period of time until we could be assigned seven seats together on a flight. Passenger seats were not obtained simply; some of these seat reservations had been worked through the Military Air Transport Service reservation system months ahead of time. And requests for transportation didn't normally come out of Nouasseur; they came from the transportation offices of the base which we had departed. We had to wait another two to three weeks before we could obtain seats for us to return to the States. What should have taken three days took four weeks. During the wait we walked around the base, spent some time in the base library, and watched movies at the base theater. Fortunately Nouasseur had a good golf course, so I was able to play a little golf.

When we finally arrived at Charleston, we pulled our car out of storage. Because we had been delayed, it had arrived several weeks before we did. Our hold baggage had arrived and had been sent on to our next base. We gathered our luggage and piled into the car. There were seven of us in the car, and I had to buy a luggage rack for the top of the car to hold our bags. Although it was an Oldsmobile, a large car, it was crowded with seven people.

CHAPTER 16

Great Falls, Montana

WHEN THE 316TH Air Division disbanded, all of the fighter pilots were sent to ground controller intercept (GCI) training. Few individuals were excepted from this order. To a fighter pilot, of course, being a GCI controller was seen as the end of the road, a dead end. The higher level reasoning was that if more pilots worked in the GCI sites, the number of incidents or accidents that occurred as a result of controller lack of familiarity with pilot procedures would decrease. And there had been problems on the intercepts: mishaps, close calls, recovery in bad weather. I was one of the pilots assigned for GCI training. I was assigned to the 801st AC&W Squadron, located at Great Falls, Montana.

When I arrived in Great Falls, I was promptly sent to GCI training. At that time the GCI system had been integrated into the SAGE system, or semi-automatic ground environment, and the school for the system was located near Kansas City. While I was waiting for an assignment for school, I spent my time going to base operations, flying whatever aircraft were there to fly—U-3s, L-1s—anything I could get my hands on to build up flying time.

I attended the intercept director course at the SAGE school, located at Richards-Gebour Air Force Base from September through December of 1960. While I was there, the promotion list was published, which indicated that I had been selected for major. By the time I returned to Great Falls, in January of 1961, I was assigned to the Air Defense sector as a senior weapons director instead of an intercept director. I had no training as a senior weapons director, but I was able to study the duties of the position, and served successfully as a senior weapons director for the SAGE system in the 25th Air Division.

After I had been in the position for a few days, I could see that the people I had been given to train were inexperienced. Two other crews had more experienced individuals assigned to them. Those with little or no GCI experience were assigned to my crew. I formed a crew from the misfits, so to speak, and worked with them until we became the number one crew in the air division. The other crews, who supposedly had the better troops, came to us to see how we were doing our jobs. We had a much better success rate than any other crew. We had an excellent reputation in the air division, and we were selected to participate in a national exercise.

I hadn't given up on my hope of getting back into fighter aircraft again, and I made it a point to talk to Col. Don Whitlow, a West Point graduate, who was the DO, the director of operations. He later became director of personnel for the Chicago White Sox. I was talking to him one day, and I said "You know, colonel, I believe the 29th Fighter Interceptor Squadron could use a little help." To my surprise, he agreed with me. "Yes, they do," he said. "I'll see what I can do." I was happy to hear this.

About six weeks later, he called me in and said, "Go on down to the 29th FIS and tell Lieutenant Colonel Murray Surratt to check you out in the F-101." I was tickled to death. I was down there in an instant. There was no paperwork, no orders; I just showed up at the squadron. I went through the ground school and flying training and soon was checked out as combat ready in the F-101.

On my first mission in the F-101 checkout program, I was in the front seat and "Rags," an instructor pilot, was in the back seat. Immediately after takeoff an aft fire warning light for the left engine illuminated. I pulled the left throttle back, kept the right engine at full power and called out to Rags, "I've got an aft fire warning light." "Roger," he said, nonchalantly. "Shut it down."

I shut the left engine down and kept full power on the right engine. Because we had just taken off, we were full of fuel and needed to burn some off before attempting a landing. We aborted our scheduled mission and circled around the field checking our instruments carefully. Another aircraft from the squadron flew up and looked us over and said we looked okay. After a while we decided to land. I brought the aircraft in on initial approach, and pitched out, making a wide pattern and keeping the airspeed up. I turned final over the threshold, held it off, and then set it down on the runway. "Good job," Rags said. I thought so too, considering I had just made a successful heavyweight single engine landing on my first upgrade ride in the front seat of the F-101. Fortunately, it was one of the very few times I had to fly on one engine in the F-101.

It wasn't long before someone called Air Defense Command headquarters to complain. Referring to me, he said, "Here's someone who's been in GCI duties only a few months and now he's back in fighters. Why can't the rest of us do that, too?" Soon more non-flying pilots began complaining. Someone in ADC headquarters checked and said that I had to spend three years as an intercept director in the SAGE system before I could be reassigned to a fighter position. For a while there was a good deal of conversation going on between our air division and the ADC headquarters. Finally headquarters said I had to serve a minimum of one year in a GCI position before returning to the cockpit. I left the 29th and went back to the SAGE building.

But it wasn't long before my year in the system as a GCI controller was completed. In September 1961 I received orders officially assigning me to the 29th Fighter Interceptor Squadron. When I reported to the squadron, I was made a flight commander, responsible for overseeing the men in my flight: scheduling them for all duties, making sure they received necessary training and maintaining flight currency.

Shortly after I joined the 29th, a headquarters team arrived to conduct an operational readiness inspection (ORI) on the squadron. I was asked to fly a T-33 to Hamilton Field, near San Francisco, California, to pick up a part for one of the F-101s; it was an important aspect of the ORI evaluation that we be able to keep our squadron aircraft flying. Because I was not yet operationally checked out in the squadron, I was not needed to fly in the ORI, but that meant I was available to fly to Hamilton Field to pick up the part. I was assigned a T-33 to fly to Hamilton and given a navigator as well, because we had to fly across a large section of the western United States to a field I wasn't all that familiar with. To top it all off, I had to fly down to California at night.

I departed Malmstrom about ten o'clock at night. We climbed up to cruising altitude, about 30,000 feet, leveled off, and were enjoying sailing along in the black of night, when once again, there was a bang from the engine section of the aircraft. The aircraft started to vibrate, and the engine temperature started to climb. I kept pulling the throttle back, but the vibrations were bad and the engine temperature continued to climb, and I shut down the engine. I began looking for a suitable field where I could perform a forced landing. As soon as I heard the explosion, I told the navigator in the back seat to give me a steer to the closest Air Force base. He checked his charts and said that the closest base was located at Mountain Home, Idaho, about 75 miles away. We declared an emergency and asked air traffic control to clear us direct to Mountain Home.

Fortunately, we didn't have any bad weather and we were able to glide towards Mountain Home without deviating from our course, arriving over Mountain Home about 15,000 feet over the base. I put the gear down using

Cecil Foster and F-101, Malmstrom AFB, April 1963.

our emergency gear lowering system and then put my speed brakes out, making two orbits over the runway before dead-sticking the aircraft onto the runway. After we landed, we discovered that the engine had lost a turbine blade, which had separated from the turbine wheel and had exited the aircraft through the side of the fuselage.

When I explained to the base maintenance personnel the nature of my mission, they said they would try to help me out. And what they did to help was unbelievable. They worked all night, taking the old engine out and installing a good one in its place. Then by nine o'clock the next morning they found a pilot to test fly the aircraft. He flew it, said it was okay, and signed it off to fly. They refueled it, and by 10:30 I was on my way to Hamilton Field. Those maintenance men couldn't have worked any harder if they had been undergoing an ORI themselves. What they accomplished was just amazing. But I didn't have time to do much more than thank those around the aircraft, because I had to hurry on down to Hamilton. I picked up the part and was able to return to Malmstrom in time to enable the squadron to maintain an above-average aircraft in-service rate.

CHAPTER 17

The Cuban Crisis

WHEN THE CUBAN missile crisis occurred in October of 1962, President Kennedy placed all military units on increased alert. We had been flying a maximum effort exercise that morning when we received an emergency recall order. When we landed, our aircraft were immediately refueled and loaded with nuclear weapons. We were told to go home and pack some clothes because we were going to deploy immediately. I raced home and filled up my B-4 bag with underwear and socks and flying clothes. I left a note for my wife and raced back to the flight line. At that time I was informed that I was in charge of a deployment of six F-101Bs that were going to Billings, Montana. Billings had been designated as a wartime emergency recovery field, but I had never been there.

Eighteen F-101s loaded with nuclear weapons were sitting on the ramp at Great Falls, including my flight of six. We just couldn't believe we were going to take off with nuclear weapons on board, as that had never been done. While we were standing around the aircraft we were ordered to climb into the cockpit and prepare to start engines. Once we were situated in the cockpit, we were told to turn our radios on and listen for further instructions. Almost immediately the command came: "Start your engines and taxi to the runway." As we were taxiing out, my backseater said, "We will never take off with nuclear weapons on board. This is all an exercise."

He was wrong. After we reached the end of the runway, we were cleared for immediate takeoff. We departed the field and checked in with the GCI controller, who cleared us to fly to Billings. The GCI controller followed us on radar as we flew to Billings, keeping us clear of other traffic. When we arrived in the Billings area there was a 900-foot ceiling with light rain, but we had no authorized let-down procedure to bring us into position over the field for landing. Fortunately, my back-seater, an excellent navigator, was able to position us with our on-board radar. He painted the field on radar, and we set up a rectangular pattern, broke out underneath the weather as we descended and landed. The runway was wet, but we landed without incident in our heavy aircraft. The flight from Great Falls was relatively brief, less than thirty minutes.

When we turned off the runway, we were told to park in front of the airport terminal building. The Billings airport was a civilian airfield. We pulled onto the ramp with our engines running, while I tried to figure out what we should do. There was no one to park us, no one to greet us, no one to tell us what we should do with our aircraft loaded with nuclear weapons, and no guards. I decided that we'd better shut down to save fuel, but I wanted to make certain the parking area was acceptable to the local authorities. Finally, the airport manager came out, and I asked, "Where do you want us to put our airplanes?"

"What are you guys doing here?" he asked.

"We were told to fly over here and wait for further instructions," I said. "We're loaded with nuclear weapons."

"Oh, my God," he said. "Well, just pick a place over there and park."

He pointed to a place where they parked civilian airplanes, small ones, single-engine and twin engine aircraft. We parked our aircraft and climbed out of the cockpits. I went over to the airport terminal and called air division headquarters. I reported that we had arrived at Billings, that all aircraft were in commission and had sufficient fuel for a short mission. The voice at the other end of the telephone said, "Get your aircraft ready to launch again, put yourselves on five-minute alert status, and have someone stand by the phone line for further instructions."

We had landed with almost a full load of fuel, because the distance between Great Falls and Billings is relatively short. Unfortunately, there were no fuel trucks at Billings with JP-4 fuel. There were no auxiliary power units (APUs). We didn't even have chocks to chock the wheels of our aircraft. We had nothing that would help us position and prepare our aircraft for another launch. We rolled up our jackets and used them as wheel chocks.

By the time I had called in to air division for instructions, six more aircraft, from Glasgow Air Force Base, Montana, had landed. I was made detachment commander, responsible for twelve aircraft, and the only personnel I had to help out were the men who had flown the aircraft in. If we had to start the engines, we would have to use internal air starts, which are normally used only in emergencies. But without APUs we had no other way to start the engines. We sat in our cockpits, ready to start engines again if necessary. Finally we were told we could get out of the cockpits and assume a 15-minute alert status.

As we sat there, we could see that our aircraft, nearly fully-loaded with fuel and weapons, were starting to sink into the tarmac. The surface of the ramp wasn't strong enough to support our heavy aircraft. We had no tugs, no means of pulling our aircraft out of the tarmac. At least we didn't have to worry about chocks any more. I went to the airport manager and asked if there were any resources available to assist us anywhere on the airport. He told us that Frontier Airlines operated a maintenance hangar and might be able to help. The folks at Frontier Airlines had a tug, and with their help and the use of some pieces of plywood, we were able to pull our aircraft out of the ruts they had made and position them on a stronger section of the parking ramp.

Our arrival made the Billings evening news reports: twelve Air Force aircraft stand at the ready at Billings airport, armed with nuclear weapons, ready to fly against the Russians, if necessary. We had no one to guard the aircraft but the crews who had flown them in. The only weapons we possessed were sidearms, .45 pistols with a small amount of ammunition, but hardly the kind of weapon to do serious damage if a small force of men wanted to rush us. I assigned different duties to different individuals. I asked one man to find us some means of getting some sleep; I asked another to see about food; I asked another to take charge of maintenance tasks, and placed another one in charge of area security. He arranged for us to take turns standing guard around the aircraft. To add to our discomfort, it was a nasty night. It had been raining all day, and it was cold.

During the night, a couple of students from a local college decided they wanted to investigate the situation for themselves. Apparently they wanted to see what Air Force airplanes loaded with nuclear weapons looked like at close range. They drove out in the dark, parked their car along the road near where our aircraft were located, and started to move through the fence along the airfield perimeter. One of the men on guard duty saw them and decided to move over closer to the road. The land where we were located on the field was higher than the area near the road, so he could get around above them before they could move too close to the aircraft.

He heard one say to the other, "Let's go up there and take a look at those airplanes." The other one said, "Will they let us do that?" And the first one said, "Don't worry. They won't do anything to us." So they started to walk up the side of the bank. When they reached the top, they started to move towards the parked aircraft. The officer who had been keeping an eye on them said, "Halt!"

One of the college boys said, "What are you going to do if we don't?

You won't shoot us." He wasn't prepared for what happened next. The officer racked his .45 and chambered a live shell. The sound, in the damp darkness, was unmistakable.

"Don't shoot! Don't shoot!" they called out.

He told them to put their arms up in the air, and then he marched them up into the building where we had set up operations. We called the sheriff, who came out and hauled these two boys off to jail. In spite of the uncomfortable conditions, we were able to maintain area security and protected our aircraft. We had nuclear weapons on board and we could not allow unauthorized people to wander around the aircraft.

I did not sleep at all the first night. The only way we could sleep was leaning against the wall or sitting in some chairs in the game room of the airline terminal. We had to man the telephone 24 hours a day, because we had no other communications. I rotated the communications duty among all the aircrew members, so that someone would be in contact with the SAGE system all night long. One officer eventually discovered that a Marine reserve outfit in town had some cots, and he arranged to borrow their cots so we could grab a little sleep on the second night. The second day we were there, the folks at Frontier Airlines provided room in one of their hangars; we now had some office space and a place to put our cots.

We were able to make arrangements with the people who worked in the airport terminal café; they let us eat there and agreed to a 35 percent discount. I explained that we had no orders, no paperwork, nothing to show why we were parked on the ramp at a civilian airport in Billings, Montana. We had no authority to spend a dime of government money or even to commit the Air Force to reimburse anyone for our expenses.

Finally, about 24 hours later, some air policemen and maintenance personnel arrived from Malmstrom Air Force Base; they brought fuel trucks with them, and we were able to top off our fuel tanks. Within 48 hours of our arrival, I felt that we were fairly well organized and could consider ourselves reasonably operationally ready. My air division vice-commander and my squadron commander flew over in a T-33 aircraft. At the time I was holding a meeting with the airport manager, the Federal Aviation Agency people in the control tower, the people from Frontier Airlines, the restaurant staff, and representatives from the city and law enforcement agencies. I was explaining who we were, what type of aircraft we were flying, what we were doing there, and that we needed assistance but had no money and no authority to commit funds. We had a requirement to stand alert at the Billings airport and we would certainly appreciate whatever help they could give us. They were very helpful. They let us borrow flood lights and a generator to provide night lighting around our aircraft.

In the middle of this meeting, my division vice-commander and squadron commander showed up. I introduced them to the group and asked them if they wanted to say anything, and they said no, I should proceed with my meeting. I reviewed what we had accomplished, and when it was all over, we walked out together. The air division vice-commander said, "I can't believe how well you've got the situation under control down here." I didn't realize how good a job they thought I'd done until I got a phone call later that evening from my squadron commander, who said, "You've done such a great job that we're going to bring you back to Great Falls. You've been promoted. You're now our squadron operations officer." I handed over responsibility for the Billings detachment to another officer and returned to Great Falls.

Our squadron operations officer was more than a little found out I was replacing him. I certainly couldn't blam idea this was going to happen. He was unassigned for a went to Glasgow AFB where he was given command o received a promotion as well. After the crisis was r rotated to Great Falls and a permanent detachment wa I was also recommended for, and received, a comme work during the crisis.

CHAPTER 18

From Great Falls to Germany

THE F-101 WAS AN EXCELLENT AIRCRAFT, reliable and dependable. But it did have its peculiarities. While I was the squadron operations officer, I was flying a mission one day with Lt. Larry Stevens flying number two on a practice intercept to a high-altitude target. We were practicing what we called "snap-up intercepts" in our F-101Bs. We flew at 35,000 feet at full power, and at the appropriate moment we would execute our "snap-up" maneuver by zooming up to the target's altitude, where we would intercept the target, complete our firing run, break left or right, and proceed back to base. On this particular mission, I had completed my intercept preparations, obtained lock-on on the target, made my snap-up, and completed my pass. But instead of diving away, I rolled into a position parallel with the target aircraft to watch Larry Stevens execute his intercept. As he pulled up to perform the intercept, he went into a "pitch-up" condition, which was one of the problems we experienced in the F-101. If we pulled back on the stick too abruptly, the aircraft would enter what was called the "pitch-up mode," in which it was basically out of control. By executing such a sharp nose up maneuver, the airflow was prevented from flowing normally across the elevators. In this condition the aircraft would rotate over the top and fall like a falling leaf, flopping around in the air.

The procedure to follow when this happened was to retard the throttles and pull the drag chute handle. Deploying the drag chute caused the aircraft to fall through the air in a nose-first condition instead of flopping around in the sky. Once the aircraft entered a condition in which the airflow was coming straight on to the nose of the aircraft, the airflow would be flowing across the wings, and especially the elevators, in a more normal fashion. With the plane in this condition, the pilot should be able to recover the aircraft, release the drag chute, and fly out of trouble.

I saw Larry pull up into his intercept and then go into the "pitch-up" condition. He called "pitch-up," fell on over, and pulled his drag chute release. He looked like he was going to recover, then went into an uncontrollable spin, then almost got out of the spin, then went into a spin again. In the meantime the aircraft was falling towards the ground at a good rate. There was a discussion between Larry and his backseater about whether or not they should get out of the aircraft. The backseater, said, "Let's eject!" And Larry said, "No, no, not yet. I think I can bring it out."

Pretty soon, as they passed through 20,000 feet, the backseater said, "I think we should eject now!" But Larry answered, "No, I think I've got it now." He eventually pulled the aircraft out of the "pitch-up" condition, pulling it out gradually so as not to enter a high-speed stall, which is what he had been doing in his previous attempts. Larry eventually leveled off at about 3,500 to 4,000 feet above the ground. He looked off his right wing and saw me flying formation with him. When we got back on the ground, he was incredulous. "How could you ever have joined up with me? And be in formation with me when I pulled out?" In 1996 we had a squadron reunion in Colorado Springs, and Larry said, "All this time I still haven't figured how you could have stayed with me through 30,000 feet of gyrating freefall."

In the early 1960s, we began hearing about military action heating up in a place called Vietnam, a place few of us knew anything about. One captain in the squadron became well-known later, when we started to fly in Vietnam. His name was Bernard ("Bernie") Fischer. At the time he had no combat experience. We were on alert duty together in the alert hangar one night, and we were discussing combat flying procedures because some pilots in the unit were about to depart for Southeast Asia. We were sitting around talking about what we might do in this or that case, and Bernie was asking me questions related to my experience in Korea. Finally Bernie said, "I just don't know what I'd do if I actually got into combat where people were shooting at me or I had to shoot at somebody else." And I said, "It will come naturally to you. You will follow the training you've been given. When the time comes to do something, you won't stop and think about it, you'll just do it. You'll react instinctively. You'll do what's right, and you'll know it's right."

A few years later, in 1966, he went to Southeast Asia and flew the A-1E, a prop-driven aircraft. While he was flying in South Vietnam, he made a daring rescue of a fellow pilot, Jump Myers, who had made an emergency landing in another A-1E. Two other aircraft provided cover while he landed on a debris-filled airstrip in the A Shau valley as the Viet Cong and North Vietnamese soldiers were shooting at him. He calmly taxied back where the other aircraft was sitting, opened his canopy so the other pilot could climb in. He then took off with Jump Myers squeezed into the cockpit. They made it out of there and landed safely, even though his aircraft received over 19 hits. He was able to get Myers out of the jaws of death. That took a lot of guts. And he did it instinctively, without hesitation. In my opinion, Bernie fully deserved the Congressional Medal of Honor he received for that effort.

Lt. Col. Surratt, our squadron commander, was reassigned to Newfoundland, and another officer from Air Defense Command headquarters was assigned to take command of the squadron. He was not the typical fighter pilot, and his leadership style was different from what the rest of us in the squadron were used to. He had a terrific ego. Not that ego is bad; you have to have more than a little ego if you're going to survive as a fighter pilot. But his personality noticeably interfered with his leadership ability. For instance, one day he went into the division commander's office and became so upset about something that he started to beat his fist on the division commander's desk. The division commander wrote him a letter of reprimand. Then the division commander called "Rags" and me into his office and told us, "One of you two will be on the station at all times. I may have to relieve the squadron commander on short notice and if I do, I will need to have one of you two take over the squadron. And don't tell anyone of this conversation."

Needless to say, Rags and I were surprised by this news. We were uncomfortable about the idea that our division commander would question the ability of the squadron commander to maintain command and control of the unit, especially when we were sworn to secrecy about the whole business. Rags and I were "shadow commanders" for the rest of the time that that officer commanded the unit. About four weeks later the individual received orders transferring him to the Far East. To my surprise, I was assigned temporarily as squadron commander. The assignment was unquestionably on a temporary basis; I was only a major, and a relatively junior-ranking major at that, and I never doubted for a minute that the job was nothing but temporary, and that some more senior officer would be brought in as commander. I held the position for about three months until Col. Carl Leo was brought in.

When he came in, he said, "You continue commanding the squadron. I'll tell you when I'm ready to take over." I thought this was unusual, but he seemed to know what he wanted. Finally, about ten days later, he said,

"Okay; I'll take over command now." He remained in command of the unit until I left for my next assignment. But before I was released from the squadron, I was told to come down to squadron operations and brief the ADC headquarters ORI team that was going to give an ORI inspection to the squadron. Col. Leo said it was my job to prepare the squadron for the ORI so that it would pass. Up to the last minute, even as my wife and I were trying to clean out our quarters so we could move, I was involved with the ORI preparation. At 0700 hours on the morning I left, I briefed the ORI team about the squadron's readiness while my wife and family waited outside in the car. As a reward for my efforts with the 29th Fighter Squadron, I was awarded the Meritorious Service Medal.

During my tenure as operations officer and then later as commander of the 29th Fighter Squadron, we never had a flying accident. We had a perfect flying safety record during the time I was there, from September 1961 until September 1964, when I was assigned to 17th AF Headquarters in Germany.

My fourth son, Ronald, had an ongoing problem after he was born at Perrin AFB. He had a problem with a bladder neck obstruction, and we had to take him down to San Antonio, to the Lackland Air Force Base Medical Center for an operation on his bladder. We had more problems with it at Westover and then at Sidi Slimane. For the first nine years of his life, it seemed as if he spent more time in the hospital than he did at home. This problem recurred while we were at Great Falls, and continued when we moved to Germany.

In Germany he went to an army hospital at Landstuhl where the doctors wanted to perform a serious operation called a colostomy, but my wife was smart enough to say that we needed to obtain a second opinion. The second doctor believed that no operation was necessary at that time and that the condition could be treated with medication. So we continued to treat him for this condition, and even though it has continued to bother him, he has been able to live a reasonably healthy, normal life.

While we were at Great Falls, our second son, Bryan, indicated an interest in attending the Air Force Academy. As part of the application process, he underwent a physical examination in the base flight surgeon's office. But the physical discovered that there was a problem with the sugar content in his urine. Subsequent investigation showed that an artery was blocking the tubes running from his kidney to his bladder. To correct the problem he had to have an operation in the civilian hospital. While he was in the hospital he came down with a staphylococcus infection and took a long time to recover from it. The operation helped to correct the problem but unfortunately meant that he was ineligible to attend the academy.

My three-year assignment in Germany as chief of the fighter branch at 17th Air Force Headquarters at Ramstein Air Base was enjoyable but uneventful. I learned much about air-ground operations, for we went on a number of exercises with the army. We held a number of tactical air control center exercises, and I performed the normal staff officer's duties at Headquarters. After I had been there for about two years I was promoted to Lieutenant Colonel, in 1966, and shortly thereafter I was assigned as the commandant of the Air-Ground Operations School, located at Ramstein Air Base, Germany. In that position I learned more about air-ground operations. I was involved in instructing and briefing officers from all the NATO countries, England, Canada, West Germany, Greece, and other allied countries not officially part of NATO, such as Iran and Iraq. While I was there, the French went from full participants in NATO to "political only" participants.

My flying duties consisted primarily of flying the T-33 as a target for aircraft of the 86th Air Division, the air defense network for the European theater. I didn't fly any of their F-102s, but I did fly as a target aircraft for their training missions a number of times. While I was there I participated in a number of special activities, including returning to the United States to observe a special weapons demonstration in the Charleston, South Carolina, area. This was an instructive and educational experience for me, because I had never been on the ground while live bombs were exploding in my immediate vicinity. I flew to England on several occasions, and I was also able to fly down to Greece and walk among some of the famed architectural remnants around the city of Athens and surrounding area.

My family and I benefited from visiting Europe. We traveled to Italy and spent a couple of weeks driving along the east coast, which we enjoyed thoroughly. We also visited the Costa del Sol section of Spain, and enjoyed that immensely. On our trip to Italy we drove through the Swiss Alps into Italy. That was an unforgettable experience; the road in many places was extremely narrow, but the local drivers didn't seem to notice. They drove their big busses and trucks without showing any concern. When we saw one of those vehicles coming we moved over to the side of the road until our car practically scraped the side of the mountain. It seemed like there was never more than an inch or two of clearance between the vehicles as they passed. Sometimes we would be on the outside of the turn and it was scary to look down that mountain side and see mile after mile of the switchbacks in the road, going down the side of the mountain. We visited Paris, Brussels, Amsterdam, Innsbruck and Berchtesgarten, as well. We were able to take advantage of many of the cultural activities that living in central Europe provided, for which I was thankful. This was my first assignment where flying was not my primary job, and not being on continual alert 24 hours a day had its advantages, especially as we were living in an environment rich in culture and history.

At the end of my tour I received orders for a new assignment and this time it was to Southeast Asia, where I was first assigned to fly RF-101s. I was a given this assignment, obviously, because the F101B was the last operational aircraft I had been current in. I called the personnel section and said, "If you will check my records, you will see that I don't belong in reconnaissance aircraft. I've never flown a reconnaissance aircraft in my life. I would like to be in F-4s." My request was processed through the system and soon a change in orders occurred, assigning me to fly F-4s. We left Germany on a train to Paris, where we transferred to another train and eventually boarded the S.S. *United States* for our return to the land of the "big PX," the United States. The trip across the ocean on the S.S. *United States* was one of the highlights of our time in the service as a family. But then it was time for me to train as a fighter pilot again in preparation for flying in Southeast Asia.

CHAPTER 19

The Route to Vietnam

WHEN I RETURNED to the United States in September of 1967, I found out I was a grandfather, because our first granddaughter had been born to my oldest son, Cecil Jr., who was living in Austin, Texas. We stopped in Austin briefly before I moved on to my next base, Homestead AFB Florida. I no sooner arrived there than I was sent to the Air Force's Survival School, located at Fairchild AFB, Spokane, Washington. After completing survival training, we drove from Florida to Austin for the wedding of my second son, Bryan. Then it was back to Homestead where I began my check out in F-4s.

The checkout program at Homestead was thorough. When I finished the program, I felt that I was fully prepared to fly combat in the F-4. My F-4 training was certainly more thorough than it was when I went overseas in the F-86. First we flew a few initial familiarization flights, in which we learned the feel of the aircraft, its handling and fuel consumption characteristics. We also flew the aircraft at supersonic speeds, without external fuel tanks, reaching speeds as high as Mach 2. When we flew at supersonic speeds, we took off, flew out over the Atlantic Ocean, climbed to altitude, and turned south, flying in afterburner, as fast as the aircraft would go. There were adjustable vanes on each of the engine intakes, and as we increased our speed, these vanes closed, restricting the amount of air entering the engines. On one flight, our aircraft experienced a stuck vane, and as we reached a speed around 1.5 Mach, the vane slammed closed with a loud bang, loud enough to make me think the engine had exploded. Fortunately, my instructor had warned me this would happen, but I still was surprised by the loud noise. We eventually reached a speed of Mach 2. When we pulled the throttles back out of the afterburner range, it felt as though we had extended gigantic speed brakes, because the aircraft slowed very abruptly. We made sure our shoulder harnesses were locked before we did so, because the deceleration threw us suddenly forward in the cockpit.

We flew day air-to-ground missions, utilizing our SUI-16 pods hung on the aircraft, shooting at targets on the ground. We dropped small bombs on the range and practiced skip bombing as well. One night I flew a mission to the gunnery range, which was located near Sebring, Florida, where my father and uncle lived. When I arrived in the area of the gunnery range, I checked in on the radio with the range officer. He said to me, "I have visitors in the tower to observe your runs," and I knew that my father and uncle had come over to watch me practice my night runs. I was pleased at the thought that my father could watch me go through my paces in this airplane, even if it was at night.

We flew some air-to-air missions, in formation, but most of our missions were air-to-ground, because that was the primary kind of activity we were going to be doing in Vietnam. My gunnery scores were in the top 20 percent of our class and my bombing scores were in the top 30 percent. Although I was not the top scorer in our class, I was relatively proud of my bombing scores, because I had never flown any air-to-ground missions before. All of my flying experience had primarily been in the air-to-air category.

The Air Force's water survival school was also located at Homestead, and I completed that school next. I didn't particularly enjoy water survival school, because I didn't consider myself a good swimmer. When I was growing up, I did not live near any large body of water, and never learned to swim. When we entered water survival school, we were asked to identify ourselves if we were concerned about our ability to swim, and I did so. I thought that those of us who indicated concern about our swimming ability would receive special consideration in our swimming tasks, but I believe that we instead marked ourselves as needing extra attention, with the result that we often had to swim more, not less, than the other people in the class. I was given a helmet to wear during water survival training that had a big white "X" on it, so that it would be easy to spot on the open water.

I enjoyed the parasailing portion of the training, except that when it came time to launch me into the air, the boat that was towing me did not have quite enough power to pull me safely through the air, and I splashed into the water prematurely and was pulled along in the water for awhile until the boat handlers stopped the attempt. An even worse experience, however, was the mechanism designed to train us to survive being pulled through the water by an inflated parachute in a strong wind. This exercise began when we were blown off a raised deck into the water by the force of the wind generated by a big fan which filled our deployed parachute with air. The fan blew us into the water where a speedboat then pulled us along through the water. The speed would cause our heads to drop below the water, and we had to spread our legs in a manner that would allow our heads to rise above the surface of the water. When my turn came, I tried to raise my head above the water, but the speedboat kept moving ahead and my head would drop below the water again. The speedboat eventually stopped, but not before I had swallowed more water than I cared to drink.

Another sequence that did not work out too well for me occurred in connection with a helicopter pick-up drill. They set us out in the water in Biscayne Bay, where we inflated our personal life preservers, or "Mae Wests," waiting our turn to be picked up by the helicopter. But the helicopter that was involved in the training developed mechanical problems after he had picked up all the students except me. There was a safety crew in a boat watching the exercise, and they came by to tell me what was going on and that the helicopter would be shortly back out to pick me up. But then I noticed that one individual in the boat got out a rifle and sat there in the boat with a rifle in his hand, as the boat stayed relatively near me, about 75 or 100 yards away. I had no idea what was going on. Later they told me that some sharks were sunning themselves in the area. Fortunately, they weren't actively feeding.

In the meantime, the helicopter, which had been repaired, brought out another load of students and dropped them into the water one at a time, and then picked them up out of the water again. Then the helicopter came out and picked me up, after I had been in the water for over two and a half hours. They had decided to revise the helicopter pickup procedures, but they wanted to conclude with an exercise in which we swam into shore from a specified distance in the water. But because I was the last one on the helicopter, I had to be the first one to go back in the water, meaning that I had the farthest distance to swim to shore. And because I was not a good swimmer, it took me a long time to swim into shore. By the time I reached the shore every other student was long gone. When I finally struggled on to the beach, I was angry. It was after six o'clock in the evening, and almost everyone had gone home for the day. I felt certain that I had been targeted for special treatment because I had that white "X" on my helmet.

I eventually completed water survival, but I didn't especially enjoy it. I'm sure that if I had been more confident of my swimming ability I would have been more successful in my training. But I have to say that I benefited from the ordeal, and gained confidence in my ability to survive in the water. In fact, when I was faced with the prospect of bailing out in Vietnam, which

I was prepared to do twice, I did not hesitate to head the aircraft out over the water to initiate my bailout procedures. Although I never did eject over water, I would have done so with confidence in my ability to survive.

Before I left for Southeast Asia, I obtained housing for my family at Salinas, Kansas, where an Air Force base had been closed but base housing had been made available for the families of military service personnel who had been assigned to Southeast Asia. Departing Salinas, Kansas, was one of the most heart-rending, difficult moments I have ever experienced. I was waiting to catch a flight out on Frontier Airlines, but the flights had been delayed that morning due to a thick fog. For some reason, when it came time finally for me to board the airplane, something in my head said, "This is the last time you're going to see your family." The thought occurred to me that I had used up all my luck in the first war I had been in, the Korean War. Those bullets that had been fired at me and missed were going to get me this time. I might have escaped safely from one shooting war, but I couldn't see how I would escape a second one. It was a mental stretch for me to walk away from my family and board that airplane. I don't think they knew how hard it was for me to leave them. I thought I was saying good-bye for the last time.

I flew to California, to Travis Air Force Base, where, only four hours later, I caught a plane for the Philippine Islands, at Clark Air Base north of Manila. The first thing I did when I arrived in the Philippines was to go through jungle survival school. The jungle survival school taught me how to survive with almost no provisions, how to use jungle vines for a variety of purposes, how to cook snake meat, and how to prepare nets to catch fish. While I was there I ran into an old friend of mine, who had been in the 324th Squadron with me at Westover and at Sidi Slimane. Norm and I went through jungle survival together, and when we completed the course he told me he had been assigned on temporary duty to a unit at Da Nang, South Vietnam, and was leaving immediately via courier aircraft for Da Nang. My orders assigned me to Da Nang too, but to the 366th Tactical Fighter Wing, not to a specific unit in the wing. Norman said, "Since you're going to Da Nang too, I'll talk to the crew and see if we can't get you on board."

As soon as we were released from the survival school, we grabbed our bags and raced to the flight line. It was late in the afternoon when we arrived, and the aircraft was ready to depart. Yes, the pilot said, they had room for me. So I threw my bags on board and flew direct from Clark Field to Da Nang. I didn't have to wait for another ride, that would have taken me to Saigon, where I no doubt would have waited a week or more for orders to proceed to Da Nang.

When I arrived at Da Nang, Norm obtained a jeep and drove me up to the operations building of the 366th Tactical Fighter Wing headquarters. I pulled out my orders and said, "I'm here." When I signed in, the airman who was on duty called the wing deputy commander for operations (DO), who came down to pick me up. "How did you get here?" he asked me. When I told him, he said that usually new personnel came through 7th Air Force Headquarters in Saigon, who then sent them on to their final destination. But my orders had said nothing about proceeding to Saigon, so I didn't. "Well," he said, "we've got to call 7th to see what they want us to do with you." When they called 7th AF there was no one around except for an airman two-striper, which wasn't unusual, given that it was the middle of the night. The two-striper said there wasn't anyone else around and as far as he knew, I could stay at Da Nang. So I did.

I arrived at Da Nang on the last day of June 1968. Our tour of duty in Vietnam was 13 months in length, and the first month of the tour was the month we signed in. By proceeding directly to Da Nang and signing in as soon as I arrived, on the last day of the month, I essentially shortened my tour by a month. I didn't plan for this to happen; it just happened.

CHAPTER 20

My First Combat
in Vietnam

AFTER RECEIVING APPROVAL to stay with the 366th TFW in Da Nang, I next had to find a place to sleep. Da Nang was overloaded with people, and there were no empty beds. Finally they located one empty bed, which belonged to a crew member who was missing in action. They told me to sleep in that bed for the night and the next day they would find a bunk for me. I didn't like the idea, but I needed a place to sleep. I bounced from one bed to another for the next four or five days until I was assigned a room in the bachelor officers quarters barracks. That barracks building was awful—there was no ventilation, no air conditioning; it was miserably hot and humid.

I was assigned for training to the 389th Tactical Fighter Squadron, and a friend of mine whom I had known from K-13 in Korea, Lt. Col. Pat Humphrey, was the commander of the squadron. I completed my check out and flew my first combat mission with the 389th. I was able to tag along while Pat ran the squadron, so I was able to see what was involved in running a squadron in South Vietnam. This was useful information to me because it had been a while since I had been in an operational squadron, and I wasn't familiar with the unique challenges of flying in Southeast Asia. In the process of flying missions under the guidance of the squadron's instructor pilots, I gradually become familiar with F-4 operations in Vietnam. I was learning also why Da Nang was called "Rocket City"—it was constantly being bombarded with mortar attacks. Fortunately the rockets tended to fall in other areas than where we were billeted, but we never knew when an attack would occur.

By the middle of July I had flown nine missions, eight of them over the southern part of North Vietnam. I saw that I was fighting a different kind of war in Vietnam than I had flown in Korea—interdiction and close air support missions instead of air-to-air missions. I began gradually to get used to the idea of receiving ground fire when I flew my bomb runs. On my first night mission I estimated that over 2000 rounds of anti-aircraft fire were sent in my direction. None hit, however, and I had the satisfaction of starting a number of fires and seeing a number of secondary explosions—meaning that I hit some ammunition on the ground.

Another lieutenant colonel had arrived the same time as I had, and we were making our way through the checkout program together. Each day we would meet at the mess hall and one of us would say, "Have you heard anything about what your assignment will be?" and the other one would say, "No; not yet." We would meet either for lunch or the evening meal. This went on for about two weeks, and our discussion was always the same: no assignment yet.

At the end of July the Wing Deputy for Operations (DO) called me into his office and said, "We're going to assign you as commanding officer of the 390th Fighter Squadron, but you can't tell anyone yet, because the man who's the current commander doesn't know about it." This seemed a little unusual to me. I had an assignment, but I couldn't tell anyone about it. Later, when I met the other lieutenant colonel in the dining hall, we had our usual conversation. I said, "Have you got an assignment yet?" he asked. "Can't say as I have," I said.

A few days later, the DO directed me to take command of the squadron. He introduced me to another lieutenant colonel and told me he would be my new operations officer. When I walked in to the squadron, the squadron commander was out flying a mission and the operations officer wasn't around. But the first sergeant was there. I walked up to him and introduced myself, and said, "I'm the new squadron commander, and I'm taking over as of now." The first sergeant did a double-take, and then said, "Yes sir." The men in the squadron had no clue that this was going to happen. The current squadron commander had held the job only for about six weeks, and had taken over the job shortly before I arrived. Apparently his actions as squadron commander had not pleased the wing commander, who had decided to replace him.

But this unorthodox method of replacing the previous squadron commander meant that I was the man in the middle; the wing commander wasn't happy with the squadron commander, and the men in the squadron weren't especially happy with me, at least not at first. When the previous squadron commander walked into the room after flying his mission, I asked him if he had been apprised of the situation. "My first sergeant just told me about it," he said. "I had no idea this was going to happen." "I didn't either," I said. I knew he had Officer Efficiency Reports to write and other administrative tasks to accomplish, and I told him to continue using his office until he was finished. Unfortunately, he took an unusually long time to close out his paperwork. In addition, he started flying two missions a day, trying to build up his combat time, because he was being transferred to 7th AF Headquarters in Saigon.

Each squadron commander shared a mobile home with the operations officer and the squadron maintenance officer. This was a convenient and useful arrangement because these three individuals could discuss squadron business without having to call special meetings or arrange for a place to meet. These mobile homes had three bedrooms, were fully air-conditioned, and included their own shower facilities. They were reasonably luxurious quarters, at least compared to the standard barracks. I enjoyed this set-up a great deal, once I was able to participate. But the former squadron commander didn't appear to be in any hurry to check out of his trailer. Two weeks after I appeared, he was still fully installed in the squadron trailer and showed no signs of leaving.

Finally I asked the Wing DO for help. I told him I needed to take control of the squadron, but the former commander was continually finding things to do to avoid leaving. The DO said he would intervene. Finally, after another week passed, the former squadron commander departed the base. I then began to get to work in earnest, working 15 to 19 hours a day, keeping track of over 60 officers, 150 airmen, and 20 airplanes.

On the evening of the 9th of August I flew an armed reconnaissance mission over North Vietnam; I was flying in the lead aircraft with my backseater and another pilot, one of the squadron's instructor pilots, was flying number two position with his backseater. We took off about a half-hour before dark. Our target area was a road in the vicinity of Route Pack One, an area in the southernmost part of North Vietnam, just across the border between South and North Vietnam. I was flying lead, and the instructor pilot in the other aircraft was evaluating my flying proficiency. Once we arrived in the area, if we saw moving vehicles, trucks, or troops, I was supposed to call out the activity, but he would make the first pass and drop his bombs, while I flew a rectangular pattern and attacked whatever target remained.

We were flying about 4000 feet above ground level when I saw some trucks parked along the road. These trucks did not look like American trucks; they weren't that large. They were smaller and odder-looking, but they were trucks, no doubt about it. I could see them parked underneath some trees along the side of the road. I called them out to my wingman, but he couldn't see them. So I led the flight away a little, and then turned back towards the road. My rectangular pattern was a little too tight and close-in. I started my dive, and I could tell I was too close because I was having to push the nose down; we were pulling some negative Gs to keep the trucks in my sight. I could see I was going to overshoot the target, so I pulled off the target without dropping my bombs and broke hard left to go around for another pass. Just as I broke left, I saw what looked like a bunch of glowing popcorn kernels coming right at me from the ground at my ten o'clock position. It was North Vietnamese anti-aircraft fire.

I flew right through the middle of this burst of ground fire. I could feel it hit the aircraft, and then I saw a large hole in the middle of my right wing. I still had fuel in my drop tanks, a full bomb load, and a full munitions load. But now I had a gaping hole in my right wing and a large fire burning from fuel pouring out of the hole. Once I started to burn, I was a very visible target. My wingman said later that it looked like every gun in North Vietnam opened fire on me. I still had control of the aircraft, however, and pulled the nose up and pushed the throttles into the afterburner setting. I asked my backseater for directions to a "SAFE" area, an acronym for Selected Area For Ejection. He told me to take heading of 235 degrees, toward Laos.

I rapidly gained speed. Both afterburners were wide open. As soon as the enemy gunners hit me with that first burst of anti-aircraft fire, my aircraft started burning; there was a trail of fire extending behind my aircraft about two to three hundred feet long. The fuel and hydraulic fluid streaming out of my right wing was burning, lighting up the night sky like a torch. By the time we turned to a heading of 235 degrees, we were at 550 knots and climbing steadily.

As I turned to the heading he had given me I could see these strange funny-looking large rock formations, called "karst," that existed in this region. These looked like a concentration of rock stalagmites sticking up in the air like spikes. The belief was that by ejecting in this area, which was located near Laos, the unusually shaped rock formation would provide protection until the rescue helicopters—the "Jolly Greens"—could come along to pick us up.

I attempted to jettison my bombs, but they refused to leave the aircraft. All the emergency warning lights were illuminated, including the fire warning lights, generator failure lights, wing fold lights and canopy open lights. The aircraft continued to burn but I continued to climb. I could now see the ocean off to my left about 30 miles, and I thought, "I'd rather be over the water than over karst if we have to bail out," and I continued climbing and turning left. As I crossed the coast line, I ascended through 25,000 feet, both afterburners going full blast. I kept climbing until I reached 45,000 feet. My wingman, who had been following me during my climbout, called to tell me that it looked like the fire had gone out, which was good news.

I still had a full load of bombs on board the aircraft, and I didn't want to make an emergency landing with a full load of armed bombs on the aircraft. I tried electronically and manually, but I just couldn't shake those bombs loose. I leveled off at 45,000 feet and headed south, flying parallel to the coastline until we reached Da Nang. At this point I contacted the tower, and told them that I had been hit, had damage to the aircraft, had a reasonably full load of fuel, and had a full load of bombs on the aircraft, and that I needed to come in and make an emergency landing.

The folks in Da Nang tower were not excited to hear that I was carrying a load of bombs. They talked to some of the folks in wing operations, who called me to make sure that I had tried every possible procedure for getting rid of those bombs. Finally, after some discussion, they all agreed that I had done all I could, and they advised me that it was my option to fly over the South China Sea and eject or come in and land. All my warning lights were on, indicating I had serious control and power problems, so I didn't know what would happen when I set up the aircraft for landing. The engine controls seemed to be operating normally, but I wasn't sure how long they would continue to do so. I decided to land at Da Nang. I angled over towards the field at Da Nang and entered a high pattern. I put the gear handle down much sooner than I would have normally, but I wasn't sure what would happen when I tried to lower the gear and wanted as much time as possible to react if anything went wrong. To my surprise, when I put the gear handle down, the gear came down normally. There was no problem. However, I was sure the flaps weren't going to behave normally, because they needed hydraulic fluid to operate, and I wasn't sure there was any hydraulic fluid remaining in the aircraft.

I entered a modified simulated flame out pattern because I knew I might have to shut down my engines at any time, and if I did I wanted to be sure I could make it to the field. I flew a 360 degree descending overhead pattern, as my wingman followed me around, prepared to call out if he saw anything wrong. I put my speed brakes out, and put my gear down. As I rolled out on final approach, I extended full flaps, but as I did so I noticed a light that indicated no flaps. The F-4 aircraft had an indicator that showed a little donut that indicated if the aircraft was set up correctly on the approach and was flying at the right airspeed. With no flaps, we were supposed to fly at a higher airspeed to adjust for the loss of lift. I was

Cecil Foster standing in the hole in the right wing of his F-4; damage was caused by anti-aircraft fire on mission of 9 August 1968.

already flying at a faster speed, much faster than normal. As I recall, my airspeed on final approach was around 225 knots. Normally we didn't touch down on the runway at an airspeed higher than 135 to 140. But at 225 knots, the donut indicator showed that I was flying the desired speed.

I knew I couldn't land at that speed, so as I approached the runway I pulled the power off. I wasn't watching my airspeed indicator when we touched down, so I don't know for sure what our touchdown airspeed was, but I do know it was in excess of 200 knots. A cable was stretched across the runway to catch our tail hook, which we dropped in case of emergency. But we weren't supposed to cross the cable at a speed in excess of 165 knots, and we were going faster than that. I held the nose off the runway as long as I could to give us the benefit of aerodynamic braking, and I tried to use the brakes a little, but too much braking at a high speed would cause the tires to blow. I dropped the tail hook, and we caught the barrier at a speed of around 180 knots. If we were going too fast, the tail hook could cut the cable like a knife, and the aircraft would continue to the end of the runway, bounce off the end of the runway, and possibly end up in a ball of fire. But the tail hook caught the cable and brought us to a stop as quickly and as smoothly as if we had been landing at a normal speed.

Once we stopped, we hopped out of the aircraft and ran a safe distance away. As we did, I could see the last of our hydraulic fluid dripping out of the aircraft. We had had enough hydraulic fluid to provide flight controls and lower the gear. If we had had to fly another two minutes, we would have been in serious trouble. The armorers came out and safety wired the bombs. When they were through, a tug towed the aircraft into the parking area. The largest hole in my right wing was 79 inches long and 17 inches wide. I was told later that it was the largest hole ever sustained in an F-4, at least in one that continued to fly after receiving it. Half of the main spar that held the wing to the aircraft was gone, blown away. My flap actuator was missing. And there were hundreds of holes in other parts of the aircraft.

When we arrived in the squadron area, I was met by the wing commander, the wing deputy for operations, the wing deputy for maintenance, and several people from my squadron. They had all heard that I had taken a hit and they came down to welcome me back. That was my initial night checkout, and because it was dark by the time I landed, it counted as a check ride. And once again, it included a major emergency, which I hoped wouldn't become a regular part of my flying program in Vietnam. By this time it was the middle of August; I had flown 29 missions, 24 over the North, and I was beginning to feel like I was in a shooting war.

CHAPTER 21

Commander of the 390th Tactical Fighter Squadron

I WAS SQUADRON COMMANDER of the 390th from the 27th of July 1968 until the day I left South Vietnam, the 7th of July 1969. The normal procedure in most fighter wings was that one man would be given the job of squadron commander for three months and then would be reassigned, and another lieutenant colonel would be given the job of squadron commander for another three month period. This policy was instituted to give as many men as possible experience in a combat commander situation. When my three months had passed, I asked my wing deputy for operations what I should do. He told me to keep doing my job. He said that if the wing commander wanted to put someone else in charge of the squadron, he would let me know. But he never did and I stayed there until I rotated back to the States.

My first operations officer had little experience as a jet pilot. He had been flying propeller-driven aircraft like C-47s most of his career, and had no fighter experience. After he had an accident landing an aircraft in the rain, he was transferred to another base where he became a base operations officer flying propeller aircraft. Maj. Robert Messerli, who had been the assistant operations officer, was temporarily assigned as my new operations officer. I worked with Maj. Messerli and trained him for some time. He was a career fighter pilot and we worked well together. The personnel office soon sent in another lieutenant colonel to replace the one who had

Cecil Foster (second from right, front row) and members of 390th Tactical Fighter Squadron, Da Nang, 1968.

been transferred, but I held off making him the operations officer until Messerli had enough time in the position for me to write an Officer Efficiency Report on him as an operations officer. I did this intentionally to provide some good OER material for Messerli so he could benefit from receiving an OER as an ops officer in a combat unit in the next promotion cycle. Messerli eventually retired as a major general.

After Maj. Messerli rotated, I brought the new lieutenant colonel into the position. Andy was originally an Australian who had been able to get a commission in the United States Air Force. Andy was a real scrounger, and he did a good job as operations officer. He was there about three or four months when a personality conflict developed between him and my wing deputy commander for maintenance, and Andy became persona non grata in the wing. Shortly after that, he was reassigned to 7th Air Force, and I was assigned another operations officer. Four operations officers worked for me during my tour in Vietnam.

Sandbags were stacked around our trailer in Da Nang, the trailer I shared with my operations officer and maintenance officer, to protect us from the shrapnel of the incoming rockets of the 188mm mortars fired by the Viet Cong into the air base at night. When the attacks did occur, they could be spectacular. During my first couple of months in Vietnam, every time there was a mortar attack I would go out and hunker down between two rows of sandbags to protect myself from the possibility of flying shrapnel. After I had been there a while, my reaction changed. By the fall of 1968, instead of diving for the sandbags, I climbed to the roof of my trailer and sat up there watching the incoming rockets as if I were watching a 4th of July celebration. Whenever the rocket attacks began, the C-47 gunship, "Puff the Magic Dragon," circled the area and fired with its rapid-firing cannon, its tracer shells looking like a steady stream of liquid fire, falling to the ground from a dark spot in the night sky, where it was circling overhead. The sight never ceased to amaze me, and during subsequent nighttime mortar attacks, I spent more time on the roof of our trailer than I did between the rows of sandbags.

By the first week of October I had flown 60 missions, 49 of them over the North. I typically flew against suspected ammunition storage sites or communications stations. On one night mission on the 5th of October I dropped a cluster of CBUs over several targets and set off 56 secondary explosions. I could see the area burning from 50 miles away when I headed south to Danang. In October the inclement weather forced us to reduce our missions; during one week, for instance, we received over 36 inches of rain. But by November the weather cleared and we flew almost every day.

At the time that I took command of the 390th, we had permission to fly into North Vietnam to bomb officially "fragged" targets, those targets approved for us to hit by 7th Air Force at Military Assistance Command Vietnam (MACV) Headquarters in Saigon. All targets in North Vietnam had to be officially approved, and the approval had to come from the White House in Washington, DC. We couldn't fly into North Vietnam on our own authority, looking for targets of opportunity. Targets in South Vietnam were typically assigned to us according to the need to support American army or South Vietnamese army actions. After I took command it became painfully obvious that we had few worthwhile targets, targets that merited the expenditure of ordnance and the risks to the aircrews associated with delivering live ordnance into hazardous territory.

Often there were no decent, militarily valuable targets. Many times we were tasked to go out and hit what we termed "the yellow brick road," the Ho Chi Minh Trail, a narrow road that wound through the mountains in the north, went down through Laos, and then came into South Vietnam in various points. Many of these trails were little more than bicycle trails, which the North Vietnamese would use with weapons strapped to their bicycles, pushing supplies through the trees to the south.

Some of our missions were totally unproductive; we would be asked to bomb a mountainside alongside a road, so that the rocks and dirt we knocked loose from our explosion would fall down onto the road, blocking the trail. Or we would be asked to bomb the roads, making craters in the roads; after we completed these missions, the North Vietnamese would come scampering out of the woods with their picks and shovels and baskets and within a few hours the holes in the road would be filled in again. Often, all the North Vietnamese had to do was push the dirt that the explosion piled up around the crater back in the crater again. The workers would smooth out the bombed spots and the traffic would begin to move along the road again. These bombing attacks along the roads constituted harassing effort, as far as I was concerned. The North Vietnamese soldiers and Viet Cong pretended to be farmers and villagers during the day, but during the night they would get their arms and engage in military or transport activities. It was difficult to maintain a positive attitude when we doubted the value of our efforts. Flying high-performance aircraft like the F-4 in this frame of mind could have an adverse effect on our flying proficiency.

We had our share of accidents. A well-qualified pilot was working with a U. S. Navy aircraft, flying on a classified mission over North Vietnam. The navy aircraft was equipped with a special infra-red scanning device designed for surveillance of the ground beneath. Infra-red devices are common now, but at that time it was a new technology. They were looking for targets on the ground appropriate for a "flare-out" procedure. Once the target was sighted, a flare was dropped, and the accompanying aircraft, two of our aircraft flying in trail, were to strike the target. The first strike aircraft was supposed to make a diving attack on the target, pull off the target, and clear the second aircraft (his wingman) in for his attack on the target. While the second aircraft was making its pass, the first aircraft was supposed to proceed off the coast and hold in a predetermined position over the water. But when the attack was initiated, the first attack aircraft, instead of proceeding over the water, apparently remained in the area to observe the results of the second aircraft's attack. In the darkness the pilot of the first aircraft apparently couldn't maintain visual clearance from the terrain; his aircraft ran into the top of a hill. Just as it hit the hill, it exploded, but the backseater was able to eject and his parachute opened in time to stop his descent before he went into the trees. He called on his radio's emergency channel, and we were able to pull him out by helicopter. The navigator survived, but the pilot didn't.

On Thanksgiving Day 1968, I was scheduled to fly an early morning mission that was scheduled to take off at 0600 (six o'clock in the morning). Prior to take off, I attended the 0400 briefing where I received the intelligence information, the target information, the routing to the target, the weather, call signs, codes, and emergency procedures. I was just about to leave the briefing area to go to my aircraft when I heard a loud boom. At first we thought that it was an incoming mortar round. But there weren't any more explosions, so we continued with the briefing. While we were conducting the briefing, we received word that one of our aircraft had just crashed on the field.

I checked the call sign of the aircraft that had gone down, but the call sign of the aircraft that had crashed wasn't one of our squadron aircraft. Then a few minutes later I learned that it was one of our aircrews, which had been flying another squadron's aircraft. We normally provided our own aircraft for our assigned missions, but if one of our aircraft was not available for a mission, we would borrow an aircraft from one of the other squadrons in the wing. Earlier that night, another squadron had borrowed two of our aircraft for a night mission. In return they had made two of their aircraft available for two of my pilots to fly early the following morning.

My two crews had departed on an early morning mission and had been working close air support in South Vietnam with friendly troops in contact with enemy forces. One of the pilots was my squadron maintenance officer. When he returned from the mission to land at Da Nang, he apparently hadn't noticed that one of his external fuel tanks wasn't feeding properly. When he started to flare just prior to landing, his right wing dropped due to the excess weight caused by the fuel imbalance. He thought he had a split flap condition. The recovery procedure for a split flap condition is to bring the flaps up, which are normally extended to slow the aircraft for landing, and give the aircraft full power. Unfortunately, he didn't have a split flap condition, and the recovery procedure aggravated the situation. When he lifted his flaps, he lost his remaining lift and control. His aircraft struck the runway with his right wing down, bounced, sheared off the right main gear, causing the right wing and right drop tank to scrape the runway. The right drop tank ruptured, and fuel started to spray out as the aircraft skidded into the concertina wire at the side of the field. The heat of the crash ignited the fuel in his tank and the aircraft exploded. The pilot was killed instantly.

As soon as the backseater saw the right wing was dragging and the aircraft was going off the runway, he ejected. But at the time he ejected, the fuel in the right drop tank, which was full, burst, spraying fuel in all directions. The fire of the ejection blast ignited the fuel, and he ejected through this ball of fire. His seat ejected successfully, his chute deployed, and he landed on the ground. Someone went up to him and asked, "Are you okay?"

He said "yes" and promptly collapsed. He had inhaled the flames he had passed through, which had burned his lungs. He survived for about two weeks at Da Nang before he was airlifted back to the States. He died enroute.

My new squadron maintenance officer was a dedicated, motivated individual who had gone through F-4 school with me at Homestead AFB, Florida. He was an extremely hard worker, and I had to send him back to his quarters on more than one occasion to get some rest because he had been working so hard. One night early in December he was out on a night mission. The night was beautiful, and the weather was clear with good visibility except for a thin layer of cloud that was covering a mountain located about four miles north of the Da Nang runway. He was returning from a mission under GCI control. He was directed to turn 45 degrees left for positive identification, and then 45 degrees to the right to return to his original course. Unfortunately, there was another aircraft in the area, a Marine F-4, who was following the same instructions and performing the same turns. The GCI people saw this aircraft on their radar scope, not my maintenance officer's airplane.

His aircraft was about ten miles behind the Marine F-4. When the Marine aircraft cleared the mountain four miles north of Da Nang, the GCI controller cleared the Marine aircraft to descend to 4,000 feet. My maintenance officer, thinking he was cleared to descend, pulled his power back, started a descent, and hit the mountain. I'm not sure why his backseater wasn't following the approach on his airborne radar; unless there was a problem with the aircraft, he should have been able to see that it wasn't time to descend yet. At any rate, the aircraft descended to 4000 feet and struck the mountain. If he had been even 50 feet higher, he might have been able to clear it, but as it was, in the cloud, he caught the top of the mountain. The aircraft hit the peak and blew up.

I went out with the helicopter the next day, but the weather was bad and we couldn't land. A day later we were able to set down briefly, and I was able to find some personal effects to positively identify the crew members. The weather closed in again, and we had to climb back on the helicopter and get out of there while we could. I wasn't able to spend as much time there as I would have liked, but we were able to confirm that it was one of my aircraft that was destroyed and one of my crews that was killed.

According to the standard military procedure, if we didn't have a body, we had to report the aircrew members as "missing in action." Initially the Air Force notified the pilot's wife that he was missing in action. His wife was living in the dependent quarters area at Salinas, Kansas, just a few houses away from the house where my wife and children were living. Somehow, his wife was able to convince some sergeant at McConnell AFB to put through a phone call to me at Da Nang. I was in my office working when one of the sergeants came in and said, "Colonel Foster, you've got a call in the ops room."

I went into the ops room to answer the call. I picked up the phone and heard my maintenance officer's wife asking me to tell her what had happened. I never felt so uncomfortable and awkward in my life. I was standing in our squadron ops room, with aircrew members, pilots and back-seaters, as well as the enlisted troops, all around me, getting ready to fly missions, talking on the telephone to the wife of one of the men who had been in that room the previous day. Not only that, I had grown especially fond of the man as a result of knowing him in the F-4 checkout program and seeing the excellent work he had done as squadron maintenance officer. I wanted to tell her everything I knew, I felt I owed it to her, but I was constrained from doing so by the circumstances, by military restrictions, as to what I could say in any form, much less over the telephone, and by my own emotions.

I told her that we didn't know for sure what had happened and that as soon as we did, I would let her know. I never felt so helpless. It was much easier for me to deal with a burning aircraft than to have to give someone bad news. It was a traumatic experience for me, first because I had just lost two fine men in what I considered an unnecessary loss, and second because I was not allowed to tell her the details of the accident, which she certainly deserved.

Every time I lost a person in combat I had to write a letter, even if it was a missing in action situation, and in the letter I had to explain as much as I legally could about the accident or incident. It was understandable that family members would want to know, "What happened? How did it happen?" I lost quite a few airplanes and men during my year in Vietnam, and I had to write many of these letters. It was never easy to do. Occasionally we had our lucky breaks. One pilot in the squadron landed with his gear up while he was carrying two armed CBU-24 bombs under the belly of his plane; he skidded along on his wing tanks until he stopped and nothing caught fire or exploded!

CHAPTER 22

Leaving Vietnam

THE NEW YEAR—1969—began for me on a relatively pleasant note, as I was able to meet Margaret in Hawaii for some R&R—rest and relaxation. We rented a car and drove to Bellows Air Force Station where we were able to secure a unit on the beach near Kailua, on the island of Oahu. We enjoyed the beautiful weather and relaxed atmosphere, drove around the island and went shopping. One of the highlights of our stay was an evening sail on board one of the Hawaiian Hilton's catamarans, where we watched the sun set over the sea and saw the lights come on along the shore. Neither one of us was especially happy when we had to part. And when I returned to the squadron, I learned there was more unpleasant news.

One of the backseaters in the 390th was Jimmy F., who went through the F-4 checkout program with me at Homestead AFB. He frequently flew in the back seat of an F-4 with a special, hazardous mission. This aircraft flew as a high-speed forward air controller aircraft in some of the more hazardous areas of Vietnam. These aircraft were called "Stormy FACs." On one particular mission early in 1969 he and his pilot were flying along the Ho Chi Minh Trail on the edge of Laos, between Laos and South Vietnam, near what we called the Mu Ghia Pass, near Techepone. They were "trolling" for guns, flying at relatively low altitude, trying to draw fire from some of the anti-aircraft artillery (AAA) units on the ground, so that when the guns fired, their locations would be spotted. The Stormy FAC would then call in other aircraft to drop ordnance on the AAA weapons.

As they were flying near the Mu Ghia Pass area, intense ground fire struck their aircraft. The plane went down, and only Jim was able to eject. The pilot in the front seat didn't survive. Jim landed squarely in the middle of hostile territory with guns and enemy soldiers all around him. This was a difficult situation for us, to rescue an aircrew member in the middle of well-defended hostile territory, and it was almost ideal for the North Vietnamese, because they knew they soon would have many American aircraft to shoot at during the rescue attempt. We discovered later that Jim had been badly injured; he was lying on top of his survival kit with an injured back, both arms and legs paralyzed. He could move only the fingers of one hand and his head.

He was able to operate his emergency radio and communicate with the rescue aircraft. The attempt to rescue him the first day failed because of the intensity of the anti-aircraft fire in the area. He lay in the same position all night, and he could see the lights from the flashlights of the NVA soldiers as they searched the area looking for him. Aircraft flew in the area all night long to interrupt the NVA search effort as much as possible. The next morning A-1Es and F-4s flew over, hoping to knock out the guns and reduce ground fire. One of the A-1E aircraft was shot down, as was the first Jolly Green helicopter crew that tried to rescue him. A second Jolly Green crew was able to rescue the first Jolly crew as well as the downed A-1 pilot. Finally, more Jolly Greens arrived and they were able to pull Jim out. He wasn't able to move, so the Jolly Green pararescue men had to go down, put him in the "basket," and pull him out. They extracted him from the area and flew him to Bangkok. When I heard that he had been rescued, I flew to Bangkok to see how he was doing.

Not too long after that incident, our ammunition dump at Da Nang blew up. Several different ammo dumps throughout Southeast Asia blew up while I was at Da Nang, usually as a result of hostile fire or enemy activity. Ours was caused by a Marine who was policing the area. He started a small fire to burn up some paper and debris. But a wind came up and blew the fire into the Marine Corps munitions dump. He thought he had contained it, but soon it was out of control. At first a few cases of ammunition started to explode. Then everything started to explode: pallets of air-to-air and air-to-ground rockets, marking rockets, 500 pound bombs, 750 pound bombs, 2000 pound bombs. Everyone on the base had to hide behind safe barriers to keep from getting hit by the metal and shrapnel that rained down on us. It was the most astounding sight I have ever seen. No fireworks celebration before or since has come close to the spectacular sound and light show that fire started. When a pallet of 2000 pound bombs exploded, the orange-red-black fireball would rise to an altitude of 4000 feet. We could see the shock waves of the explosions in the air as they came towards us.

The shrapnel fell like rain, but a very hard rain and potentially extremely dangerous. Our squadron aircraft were sitting on the flight line in reinforced covered hangars, and I went out periodically to ensure that our aircraft were in flyable condition. I say periodically, because the ammunition dump exploded for two days. When the Marine ammo dump went up, portions of the burning explosives went over in the Army munitions area, and that started to blow. Then the fallout from that conflagration fell into the American and South Vietnamese air force and army ammunition dumps. It took two days for that particular set of dominoes to fall into one another and as they did, it was spectacular. All five ammunition dumps blew sky high. And to think that that damage was caused not by the Viet Cong but by one meticulous Marine.

On the second day, when I was standing out near the flight line, one of the special canisters that held the 20mm machine gun ammunition pods that we put on the F-4 cooked off. When it went, we heard this brrrrrrrrt! and the sound of bullets whistling past overhead. I was standing near my pickup truck near the point where the taxiway entered the squadron parking area when this happened, and the minute I heard that brrrrt! I hit the ground. Those bullets sounded like they were passing awfully close overhead. But no one was hit. We and many other units at Da Nang were without munitions for a few days, and we had to fly south to other bases to load munitions on our aircraft. After the area had cooled off, more munitions were brought in and business returned to normal. Well, normal for Vietnam.

On the 2nd of April, 1969, I was assigned to fly a two-ship mission in the tri-border area, where the borders of Laos, South Vietnam, and North Vietnam joined. Needless to say, it was a dangerous area to fly over. It was my 138th mission. My task was to bomb a mountain road under the direction of a forward air controller, who was supposed to mark an area for me to bomb with his smoke rockets. There was heavy weather in the area, and I told my wingman to stay at altitude while I dropped down to see what kind of visual clearance we had on our run in to the target. If I had room I would make my pass and then my wingman could come down and make his run. As we came into the area, every once in a while there would be a clear patch where we could see the ground underneath. The FAC marked a spot in the road, and I made a rectangular pattern in the weather. I rolled out on a final heading, dove down underneath the clouds and saw where the FAC's mark was, adjusted my sights, and dropped two bombs. When they released from the aircraft I pulled up and went back into the clouds. I entered another rectangular pattern to make another run to drop my remaining bombs. I descended from the clouds for my second run. As I descended the FAC told me that my first bombs were close to the target area but that I should drop this time about 50 yards to the right of the first drop. But just as I rolled in on the target, I was hit by anti-aircraft fire. I never saw it coming, but I knew that I had been hit when the AAA projectile exploded with a loud bang and holes suddenly appeared in my right wing. I continued my run in to the target, dropped my remaining four bombs, and started an afterburner climb.

The hit caused almost exactly the same damage as I had received on my night checkout over North Vietnam. I started trailing fuel out of the holes in my right wing, which immediately started to burn. All the warning lights came on. As they say, it was deja vu all over again. As soon as I took the hit, I asked my backseater, Lt. Joe McMahon, for a heading toward the South China Sea. I had climbed to 22,000 feet and we were about 30 miles from the ocean when the engine temperature started climbing and the forward fire warning light illuminated. I knew we had serious trouble. The engine and aircraft were about to blow up. Thinking fuel might have pooled in the gear well areas, I retarded the throttles, extended my speed brakes, and dropped my gear. But the fire did not diminish, and suddenly I lost all hydraulic power. The aircraft was no longer controllable. Trying to put it on autopilot temporarily only made the situation worse. I said, "Joe, it's time to go."

We had previously agreed that in case we had to bail out, we would count one, two, three, and both pull our ejection handles simultaneously. But when I reached the count of two he was gone and I was right behind him. In the F-4 the backseater ejected first so as not receive the brunt of the fire and flame from the shell that fired the front seat out of the aircraft. The shells that fired the ejection seat were 188mm mortar shells and they expended a terrific burst of fire. When the shells fired, the crewmember experienced instantaneous G forces of about 21 Gs, or 21 times the normal force of gravity. We left the airplane at about 22,000 feet and both ejected safely. We freefell to an altitude of 12,500 feet, when our parachutes opened automatically, triggered by the barometric device attached to our harnesses. Once the parachute opened, I felt a bit of a jolt and then looked up to make sure that my parachute panels were intact. One of my panels was torn badly, but it did not interfere with the operation of the parachute. While I was falling, I saw our aircraft, still burning, roll slowly over and dive into the ground.

We were floating down through the air about 30 miles inland from the coast and 45 miles southwest of Da Nang. My wingman circled around us as we descended. I pulled my emergency radio from my survival vest and told both my wingman and the FAC that Joe and I had bailed out. Even the FAC had caught up with us in his slower aircraft, because it was easy to follow the smoke trail we had left through the sky. The FAC called GCI and told them an aircraft was down and the aircrew needed to be picked up. It just so happened that two Jolly Green rescue helicopters were flying in the Da Nang area. Seventh Air Force cleared them to head towards the location where we were going to land. The A-1Es were notified, were scrambled, and soon appeared overhead in case they were needed for ground fire suppression.

I tried to slip my parachute, by pulling on the appropriate risers, to drift over to where my backseater was going to land, but I was unable to move any closer to him than a half-mile. I saw that I was going to be landing in some trees, and I stowed my radio in preparation for penetrating the tree branches. We had been taught to cross our legs and wrap our arms around our chest prior to entering the trees, and this is what I did. I slipped down through the branches until my canopy caught on some of the branches, and for I while I swung suspended in the air, about 75 feet off the ground. The tree must have been 200 feet high. I hung there for a few minutes, until I noticed the circulation to my legs was being cut off by the parachute harness. I loosened my harness to let the blood flow into my legs more freely, and then tried to decide how I was going to get down on the ground without hurting myself.

When the A-1Es checked in with us on the radio, I told them I hadn't heard any movement in the vicinity, and Joe said he hadn't either. The Jolly Green rescue helicopters picked Joe up without a problem, but they couldn't find me, so I had to talk them over to my position. I was still hanging in a tree about 75 feet above the ground, which presented a problem, because there was only about 200 feet of cable on the Jolly Green's tree penetrator. As the Jolly Green attempted to lower its tree penetrator cable far enough to reach me, the downdraft from the helicopter blades caused my parachute to balloon out momentarily, causing me to settle down towards the ground. As I settled farther down into the tree I was able to climb out of the tree using the parachute and parachute cords and a vine that was growing around the tree trunk. Finally I was able to reach the ground, and I walked out from under the tree to find a clear area. But there wasn't much clear area, because there was a steep ravine close to the tree.

I stood on the edge of the ravine while the helicopter tried to lower the penetrator cable to me. The helicopter descended over the ravine area while the pararescue man, the PJ, leaned way out of the helicopter and began swinging the cable back and forth towards me. He had to hang way out of the helicopter to do it, without a parachute or any kind of visible restraint. He was able to swing it in towards where I was standing, and I grabbed the device, lowered the two prongs at the base, which served as a kind of seat, jumped on, and wrapped my arms around the cable.

The helicopter started to pull me up, but the cable started to swing again. I swung away from the tree when the helicopter started to pull me up, then I started to swing back towards that tree, and I was afraid I was going to hit it hard enough to do me some damage or knock me off the tree penetrator. But just at the right time, that helicopter crewman stopped the retrieval movement so that when I hit the tree I just bounced off it. When I bounced away from the tree the helicopter once again pulled me right on up out of there. They pulled me up to the door of the helicopter, swung me out a little and then swung me in and on board the helicopter. While the rescue operation was going on, I could hear a dog barking about a half mile away, and I was sure that the dog was with a Viet Cong group coming to find me. However, I never heard any shots fired, and no shots were fired by any of the rescue aircraft, so our recovery was accomplished without any exchange of gunfire. The ride back to Da Nang was a "champagne ride," one of the best I ever had in Southeast Asia.

When I returned to Da Nang, I was met by the wing commander, the deputy for operations, and several other wing and squadron members, who wanted to find out what had happened and to see what kind of condition we were in. After a quick debriefing, we climbed into an ambulance and were driven to the hospital, where the flight surgeon checked us over. He couldn't find anything seriously wrong with us, so we were released to return to our barracks. I did receive a few injuries and bruises as a result of the ejection and bailout. I had a cut on my forehead and I cut my tongue. I think I cut my tongue when I tried to say "three!" during the ejection, and my teeth cut into my tongue. After I returned to the squadron area I became unbelievably sore. My rib muscles must have been pulled out of their normal position by the force of the ejection, because I could hardly breathe the next morning. I was so sore I couldn't lie down, I couldn't walk, and I couldn't take a deep breath. I was miserable. It took several days to recover from the ejection soreness.

Five days after that ejection I had a week of leave scheduled and met my wife once again in Hawaii. When I stepped off the airplane to meet my wife in Honolulu I was still stiff and sore. Margaret and I spent most of our leave at Bellows Air Force Station once again, sitting on the beach in our swimming suits, watching the waves and the birds, eating good food, and enjoying each other's company. We drove around the island of Oahu, shopping and visiting the sights. When we went to church we were a little surprised to see that the Hawaiian custom of dressing up was to wear colorful short-sleeve shirts and casual pants. When my leave was over, I hopped on an airplane and flew back to Da Nang to complete the remaining months of my tour in Vietnam.

Cecil Foster shortly after rescue and recovery after bailing out of his F-4, 2 April 1969, near Da Nang, South Vietnam.

Once again when I returned to the squadron, I found bad news waiting for me. One of my new pilots had disappeared. He was a well-liked, exceptionally competent pilot. His flying skills were considered excellent; he had over 2000 hours in the F-4. He had 1000 hours more time in the aircraft than any other man on the base, possibly in all of South Vietnam. He was checking out as a new pilot in the squadron, flying on the wing of a man who had also flown with me in the 29th Fighter Squadron at Malmstrom. On this mission the check pilot was flying the lead position in a two-ship formation, on an in-country mission over an area located about halfway between Da Nang and Saigon.

There were thunderstorms in the area and the weather was bad, so the flight leader carefully led the flight down under the clouds. Once he leveled off, he saw that there just wasn't enough altitude available, not enough clearance under the cloud base, to do the mission right. The flight leader decided the mission couldn't be done safely, called the number two aircraft to join up on his wing, and started to climb up through the weather. When the flight leader broke out on top of the weather, his wingman, this well-qualified pilot, wasn't there. There had been no radio call, no explosion, no fire could be seen on the ground, no evidence of an accident. It was as if the second aircraft had disappeared by magic. We never heard anything more about the aircraft or the men who had been flying it.

About six weeks before I was due to rotate, around the first of June, I learned that a new squadron was coming over from the States equipped with new aircraft, F-4Es. I learned also that I had been selected to be the new squadron commander of that squadron and, to be around long enough to have an impact, I was going to be involuntarily extended for three months in Vietnam, from July until October. I was supposed to turn command of my squadron over to my operations officer. The plan was to place experienced people from my squadron in various positions in the new squadron so that there would be some experienced old heads in lead positions in this new squadron.

However, a major incident occurred in Korea just then, and instead of being sent to Vietnam, the new F-4E squadron was diverted to Korea. This last-minute change happened the day prior to the squadron's scheduled arrival in Da Nang. We had already held our change of command dinner, complete with toasts and speeches, and I had moved most of my possessions out of my squadron commander's trailer into another trailer. The next morning I got the word: the new squadron wasn't coming, and I was remaining in command of the 390th TFS. I asked the wing deputy for operations if I could count on going back to the States on my previously scheduled rotation date, in July. After checking up the chain of command, he indicated to me that I could plan on returning to the States as originally scheduled. I received orders which established my return date to the United States as the 7th of July, 1969. But then, on the 6th of July, we received word that the F4-E squadron was coming to Da Nang after all, and would be arriving on the morning of the 7th, the day I was scheduled to rotate out. I was certain that someone would try to put the old plan in effect, and that I would be asked to take over the squadron when it arrived. But I had flown 183 missions, and I was ready to head home. And I was pretty sure that not everyone knew that I was rotating on my original rotation date. I certainly didn't want to remind anyone about it.

On the morning of the 7th of July, at 0800, I signed out of the squadron and went over to the Da Nang "repple depple," replacement depot, where I waited three hours for my flight out. I didn't want to be extended at the last minute. I climbed on board the aircraft and didn't relax until the gear came up and the aircraft turned east over the South China Sea.

CHAPTER 23

Into Retirement

WHEN I RETURNED from Vietnam in 1969, I visited Wilford Hall, the large medical facility located near Kelly Air Force Base. Many soldiers and aircrew members who had been injured in Vietnam were brought to Wilford Hall for care and rehabilitation. One of these was the Lt. Jim F., who had been a backseater in my squadron in South Vietnam and who had received serious injuries a few months earlier. When my wife and I walked in, we were pleased to see that he was making a remarkable recovery. His back injury had healed successfully and he was walking. One arm and one hand were still giving him trouble, but the physical therapists were working with him regularly to improve his arm and hand movement. Later I wrote a letter for him certifying that he had in fact been shot down over hostile territory and had lost all personal effects that he had carried with him on the aircraft. At one of our 366th Tactical Fighter Wing reunions many years later, he was the featured speaker. We now refer to him as "Doctor" Jim, because once his rehabilitation was complete, he determined to complete medical school and become a part of the medical profession, a wonderful and amazing conclusion to what could have been a very unhappy story.

During a 30-day leave, I moved my household goods from Salinas, Kansas, to the upper peninsula of Michigan, for my new assignment as operations officer of the 62nd Fighter Interceptor Squadron, an F-101 squadron at K. I. Sawyer Air Force Base. I visited K. I. Sawyer first to determine the status of the unit and the housing situation. I also visited many of my Michigan relatives whom I hadn't seen for many years—my brothers and sisters, cousins, uncles, and aunts, most of whom were located in the Midland, Michigan, area.

I took my family with me to Tyndall Air Force Base, Florida, for two months while I regained currency in the F-101. I still had three sons at home. One son, Ronald, had to leave one high school and move to another during his senior year. But he was used to moving; he attended four different high schools during his high school years. Rodney attended three different high schools, and David attended two. At K. I. Sawyer I was replacing the former operations officer, who had orders to report to another unit. He used to work for me. When I was in the 324th Fighter Squadron in Massachusetts, he was my assistant flight commander. I thought it was unusual that I would replace him.

After a period of time, the squadron commander was promoted to the position of Air Division vice commander and moved to Duluth, Minnesota. I was designated as the squadron commander of the 62nd Fighter Interceptor Squadron. We had an excellent squadron safety record; I lost no airplanes and we had no accidents. We passed all inspections with flying colors. We were doing our job well, and everything was fine until we received orders to deactivate. The Air Force was undergoing a major deactivation program at this time, and we completed our deactivation early in 1971. We fixed up our aircraft in the best possible condition and transferred them to an Air National Guard unit at Duluth, Minnesota. Later we received a letter from the ANG group commander complimenting us on the fact that the aircraft had been delivered in excellent working condition and appearance. All of us received reassignment orders, and mine was to report to McChord Air Force Base in Tacoma, Washington.

I went to McChord as the director of fighter operations, 26th Air Division. But once I had been there, a full colonel was assigned and I had the job of training him to be my boss. Once he was trained, he became the director of fighter operations and I became his assistant. I was assigned to fly the T-33 to maintain my flying proficiency, and while it was a fun airplane to fly, I missed flying first-line aircraft. I had been asked to become commander of the 4628th Air Defense squadron at McChord, but for a while I resisted. Finally I accepted, and for two years I served once again as a squadron commander.

In working with the enlisted personnel in the squadron, I tried to improve morale and efficiency, and I discovered that it was important to document all administrative and disciplinary actions. For example, two enlisted men in the squadron had been accused of using illegal drugs and had been disciplined appropriately. They wrote to their fathers, who then wrote to their congressmen, and a congressional investigation took place to see whether or not I was exceeding my bounds in the way that I was treating my people. The investigation showed that I had treated their cases fairly and all actions had been well-documented. The men were indeed guilty of using drugs and they had largely been fabricating stories to get themselves out of their punishment. I had relatively little difficulty with men using drugs, because I made my policy clear: drug use was a punishable offense, and if any man was caught using drugs, he knew what the punishment would be.

After a while it became evident that it was time for me to retire, and I used the last two years of my four years at McChord to prepare for retirement fiscally and, most importantly, mentally. I had noticed that many people who retired from the Air Force and attempted to transition from a stressful job into inactivity, went into depression or had physical problems of some kind. Many people just weren't prepared for retirement. Some even committed suicide. Many died within six months of retirement. I determined I didn't want to have these kinds of problems, and I prepared myself as best I could.

All of my children had completed college except for my youngest, David, who was in his junior year at Redlands University in California. I bought a new travel trailer and a brand new truck that could pull heavy loads and made arrangements to go on a long, extended vacation, of the kind that I'd never really had the opportunity to enjoy the entire time I was in the Air Force. When I retired, I signed out, and Margaret and I stepped into our truck and headed south, to southern California. Margaret and I spent about a month in California, visiting one son in college and one in theological training. Then we visited another son in Salt Lake City, and then drove the trailer to Michigan and visited members of my family. We drove on to Washington, DC, via Hershey and Gettysburg, Pennsylvania. Then we drove to Virginia and North Carolina, where we visited some of the early settlement sites and I learned a lot about history, more meaningful than the history I had learned out of history books in my younger days.

Next we drove to Georgia, where my oldest son, Cecil Jr., was on active duty as a lawyer in the Army, then down to Florida to visit my dad and another sister. We returned to Georgia in time to see our first grandson born. We concluded our travels at Williams Air Force Base, Arizona, where I had earned my pilot wings back in 1948. We parked our travel trailer in a mobile home court in Chandler, Arizona, for the rest of the winter. The following spring we drove up to Salt Lake City, where I had placed our household goods in storage. We first rented a two-bedroom apartment but it was too small to hold all our furniture; there was hardly any room to move around.

After traveling around the country for over a year my wife and I finally decided to settle near St. Regis, Montana, where I built a house on some

Cecil and Margaret Foster, 50th wedding anniversary, 1995.

land I purchased on the Clark Fork River in the Lolo National Forest. Working with a contractor in the area, I spent two years building our home on the Clark Fork River. This was a totally enjoyable experience, one of the highlights of my life. It was probably one of the best houses ever built, because I made sure that nothing about it was wrong. If something was done incorrectly, it was redone correctly.

On Memorial Day of 1997 I was invited to return to Midland, Michigan, where I was the Grand Marshall of an American Legion-sponsored parade. I received several awards from the city, county, and state officials. I donated several items to a museum in Frankenmuth, Michigan, a museum called "Michigan's Own," which features displays about Michigan military veterans. A display booth describes my achievements and includes one of my uniforms and some other items. One of the objects on display there is a piece of the first aircraft that took hits while I was flying in Vietnam, the fairing that covered the umbilical cords down to the bombs and the drop tanks. It is a fabulous museum!

I'm a member of the American Fighter Aces Association and have attended some of their meetings. A new museum is being established, near Seattle, Washington, and I will be providing additional items from aircraft that I've flown. An F-86 Sabre Pilots Association meets in Las Vegas every two years, and I'm active in that organization, which is dedicated to perpetuating the history of the F-86s by the pilots who flew it.

I often speak to school groups, elementary, middle schools, and high schools. I've written articles for several publications. I was ordained a deacon in the Gilbert First Baptist Church in Arizona and served there for seven years. I was a church elder in the St Regis Community Bible Church in Montana and served there for five years. I've taught Bible studies in Sunday school, and we participate in visiting an Elder Care Nursing Home in Las Vegas. When I was stationed in Germany in 1967 I joined the Masonic Lodge, passing the examination for the 3rd degree just two days before we returned to the United States. I continue to be associated with the Masons, and I especially enjoy the work the group does in helping unfortunate and disadvantaged children. Although Margaret and I certainly had some difficult times trying to keep our own children healthy as we moved around during my career, I am thankful that our family has grown and prospered. In addition to our five sons, at present, Margaret and I have twelve grandchildren, and three great grandchildren.

On the 18th of October 1991, I was living in my Clark Fork River home when my heart stopped. Shortly after it stopped, I passed out. It had stopped and started numerous times in the previous four days. I had gone to a family doctor who didn't recognize what had been happening. Fortunately, after I passed out, my heart started again and I revived. My wife was able to get me into our car and we drove to a neighbor who drove me to a hospital about 25 miles away, and they in turn airlifted me by helicopter to Missoula. There I had a pacemaker installed. I had a subsequent successful heart operation replacing my aortic valve in the summer of 1999, and have been going strong ever since.

CHAPTER 24

Looking Back

WHEN I CAME into the service in 1943, I was a part of the United States Army. The Air Force had not yet come into existence. Our flight technology was almost primitive compared to the technology of today. We thought that bombers that carried 5,000 pounds of bombs and fighters that flew faster than 300 miles an hour were the best there were. We thought that engines with 16 in-line cylinders were the ultimate in design and speed. The idea that we could travel at supersonic speeds or incorporate stealth technology was simply incomprehensible then. I first learned to navigate by using hand-held sextants to take sun shots, star shots, or by looking out the window reading a map. We used to estimate the wind by using a drift meter and navigate using dead reckoning navigation techniques. Now we have global positioning satellite systems to tell us where we are.

In weapons systems, we have gone from "dumb bombs" to "smart bombs," from bombs that worked only as well as our ability to drop them accurately on a target to laser-guided, flyable munitions. Using aids like radar and satellite-based systems, we have been able to improve our accuracy from hundreds or thousands of feet to less than ten feet. It really is amazing to think about how much change has occurred in aircraft and weapon development.

Comparable to the changes in technology in the Air Force are the changes in the personnel we have in the Air Force. When I first entered the Army, it was rare to see a woman or a member of another race in uniform. Integration was an important aspect of Air Force growth. I believe that a man should be judged on his capabilities and performance, not on any external physical characteristics. Whenever I was a squadron commander, the members of my squadrons knew that there were no "second-class citizens." Our aircrews included pilots and navigators and weapons systems operators. We were all officers and we all had our jobs to do. If we were to be successful as a unit, everyone had to do the job well. In the F-4D, for instance, the backseaters functioned as an extended set of eyes and ears, and if they didn't do their jobs well, the crew was not a complete, coherent, well-functioning entity. It would be like a human body trying to function without eyes or ears.

The same philosophy applies to the ground and support personnel as well: the crew chiefs and the maintenance personnel are essential to the success of the flying mission. They should be treated as well as the flying personnel, for without their cooperation and hard work, the mission will not be accomplished. Without a well-functioning team, the job won't get done. We all have skills at which we excel. No one is lacking in merit. It's just a matter of finding that skill and developing it and putting it to good use. Working with another person requires mutual listening and understanding of the individual's concerns and motivations.

On the subject of including women in the armed forces, I wish I could be more enthusiastic. But I have serious reservations about mixing genders in the combat environment. Problems can arise when men and women are mixed together in close quarters. There are few problems when many personnel are working together, but when we look at situations where men and women are in isolated or remote locations, working under unusual pressures, it seems almost impossible to avoid sexual relationships that can work against the best interests and coherent operation of the unit.

If there is one area where I believe we could improve our situation, that is the area of inter-service cooperation. Even though we have a number of programs where we try to educate ourselves about how the other services do their jobs, I believe that we still to a large extent fail to understand how other services accomplish their specific taskings.

As my service career shows, a determined individual with relatively little privileged background can succeed in the service. My success story, and I think it can be called that, shows that regardless of the conditions in which we begin our lives, if we set goals and work towards them, we can achieve anything we set our minds to. I really believe it. No service career is without its ups and downs, but if you have a vision of what you want to do, you will get there. Since I retired from the Air Force, I often speak to students in schools, and I try to impress upon them that if they work hard in school and educate themselves, and learn the most they can possibly learn in school, they'll learn to apply themselves successfully in spite of their background or family problems. Nobody could have started from a less advantageous position than I did in my life. I doubt that many other people suffered through the same amount of poverty, distress, and childhood diseases as I had, had their families disrupted by death or poverty, or were shuttled as frequently from one location to another. It is important to realize that unpleasant circumstances can be worked through, given individual determination and time. If we put our hearts in it we can reach our goals, regardless of conditions.

I've had the kinds of success that many people dream about. I've had a good career in the Air Force, and I've achieved a variety of records in the Air Force flying a variety of aircraft. I began as a private and retired as a lieutenant colonel. That to me is quite an accomplishment for someone who, when he entered the service, knew little else except how to raise potatoes and beans and run a farm.

I've published articles and books, I've been honored in parades, I've established a sound financial base for myself, and I've been able to see my family grow and prosper. I have five sons who hold a variety of advanced academic degrees. I've even scored two holes-in-one playing golf. It is important to remember at all times that regardless of the things we realize we can't do, we should focus on the things we can do. If we follow that simple guideline, we can succeed in whatever we choose to do.

Military History
of Cecil G. Foster

CECIL FOSTER ENTERED the Army Air Corps as an aviation cadet in August 1943. Foster initially earned his navigator wings in February of 1945 and served for most of the remaining months of World War II as a radar-navigator-bombardier instructor at Pyote Army Air Field, Texas. He then entered the first class of pilot training students to graduate as Air Force pilots, graduating from Williams Air Force Base, Arizona, in February of 1947. While in pilot training, he flew P-80s, thus qualifying as one of the first jet pilots in the Air Force. He was subsequently assigned to the 66th Fighter Squadron in Alaska. Foster left the service for approximately a year and a half, re-entering the Air Force as part of the Korean War force build-up.

After completing F-86 training, Foster joined the 16th Fighter Interceptor Squadron, which was part of the 51st Fighter Interceptor Wing, located at Suwon, Korea—more familiarly known as K-13. Foster flew with the 16th FIS from June of 1952 through January of 1953, and was credited with shooting down nine MiG-15 aircraft and damaging two others. In recognition of his outstanding flying abilities, he was appointed a flight commander and awarded a spot promotion to the rank of captain. Foster was one of only 13 American pilots to be credited with nine or more kills flying in Korea.

After returning from Korea, Foster flew F-86D aircraft with the 3558th Flying Training Squadron at Perrin AFB, Texas, and the 324th FIS at West-over AFB, Massachusetts. At Westover he was a flight commander and an assistant operations officer. In 1958 the 324th was transferred to Sidi Sli-mane AB, Morocco, where Foster became chief of the tactical evaluation section of the 316th Air Division. Foster was then assigned as an intercept officer with the Great Falls (Montana) Air Defense Sector. Promoted to major, he was appointed flight commander in the 29th FIS, flying F-101 aircraft. During the Cuban crisis of 1962, he assumed command of a deployed detachment and was later assigned as squadron operations officer and squadron commander. In September 1964 he was assigned to 17th Air Force headquarters, in Ramstein, Germany, where he was made chief of fighter operations, and, later, commandant of the Air-Ground Operations School.

At the completion of this assignment, Foster completed F-4 training at Homestead AFB, Florida, prior to proceeding to Southeast Asia. He was assigned as squadron commander of the 390th Tactical Fighter Squadron, located at Da Nang, South Vietnam, from July of 1969 through July of 1970. During his tour in Southeast Asia, Foster flew a total of 168 combat sorties, 63 of which were flown over North Vietnam. On two of those missions, Foster received substantial damage to his aircraft. In one instance he was able to recover the aircraft safely. In one case, however, he and his backseater had to eject from their aircraft; both were recovered safely.

Upon returning from Southeast Asia, Foster was assigned to the 62nd Fighter Interceptor Squadron at K. I. Sawyer AFB, Michigan. After that squadron was phased out, he moved to McChord AFB, Spokane, Washington, where he was first director of fighter operations for the 25th Air Division, and then commander of the 4628th Air Defense Squadron. He retired in 1975. Foster accumulated over 5000 hours of flying time, mostly in fighter aircraft (F-86E, F-86D, F-101, F-4). He is a veteran of three wars and underwent extensive training for the cold war. In recognition of his airmanship and many years of distinguished service, he was awarded over 20 decorations, including the Silver Star, Distinguished Flying Cross, Air Medal, Air Force Commendation Medal, National Defense Service Medal, Korean Service Medal, Vietnam Service Medal, Republic of Vietnam Campaign Medal, Bronze Star, and Purple Heart.

Index

149